how2become

How to write a book, get it published and keep ALL the profits...

Richard McMunn

Orders: Please contact How2become Ltd, Suite 3, 50 Churchill Square Business Centre, Kings Hill, Kent ME19 4YU. You can also order via the e mail address info@how2become.co.uk.

ISBN: 978-1-910202-05-0

First published in 2014 by How2Become Ltd

Typeset for How2become Ltd by Anton Pshinka.

Printed in Great Britain for How2become Ltd by Bell & Bain Ltd, 303 Burnfield Road, Thornliebank, Glasgow G46 7UQ.

CONTENT

"You need no qualifications or prior experience to write and self-publish a book. All you need is an idea, hard work, determination and a willingness to learn..."

"Write a book that oozes quality. When writing your book focus on the reader and how it will benefit them. Do not focus on how much money the book will make for you..."

"When writing your book think about the different opportunities to upsell..."

Richard McMunn
Award-winning entrepreneur and best-selling author

WELCOME

Dear author,

It gives me tremendous pleasure to bring you this book, which is a collaboration of many years' hard work, determination and a willingness to learn.

As you read the book you will notice that in order to write and self-publish your book you need no prior experience of the publishing world. What you do need is a willingness to learn and a mentor (someone who will help you). In order to make the book interesting and inspiring I have written it from the heart. I will share with you my successes along with the many lessons I have learnt along the way.

I must stress that the methods I am going to teach you within the book are not the only way to get your book finished and published – they are simply the methods that I have tried and tested and the ones that have worked for me. You will also notice in the book that I urge you not to go out and get a book publishing deal with a major or independent publisher. The reason for this is simply because I believe the effort it takes to get a book publishing deal can be better channelled into doing it yourself. In essence, if you follow the steps and guidance I have provided within this book you will be able do it yourself. In many cases you will probably do a better job than some of the major publishers that are out there.

Finally, after reading my book if you would like me to coach you on a one-to-one basis to get your book published, please contact me via the following website:

www.RichardMentorMe.com

Good luck and best wishes,

Richard McMunn

CHAPTER 1
NO PREVIOUS EXPERIENCE REQUIRED

Get instant access to over 32 hours' worth of online training videos and support at:

www.BookPublishingAcademy.co.uk

NO PREVIOUS EXPERIENCE REQUIRED

Most of you who read this book will probably have no idea who I am or the journey I have taken so far. Therefore, in this chapter I would like to take a few minutes of your time to explain what I have done and where I have come from. This opening chapter is designed to inspire you to write your first book and to instil the belief that absolutely ANYTHING is possible.

To cut a long story short, I grew up in Lancashire and attended Balshaw's High School in Leyland, where I graduated with the princely sum of just 3 GCSE's. For all my effort, or probably lack of it, I achieved a B grade in Art, a C Grade in English Language and a C Grade in English Literature – not much use to anyone if we are being honest! Because of my lack of qualifications I decided to join the Royal Navy as an aircraft engineer. I served on-board HMS Invincible and got to travel the world whilst getting paid a decent amount in the process. However, it wasn't all plain sailing though (excuse the pun), as I did actually fail the initial Royal Navy medical for being overweight, and as a result my application was rejected until I had 'slimmed down' a little!

I can actually vividly remember attending the Royal Navy medical in Preston, Lancashire. I sat in the doctor's surgery waiting room and was confident that I would pass. I entered the room and was asked to undress. After a few minor checks and the inevitable 'cough and drop' I was told to stand on the weighing scales. This was the first time I'd ever stood on weighing scales in my life. As soon as I took that life-changing step onto the weighing scales I could hear the cogs struggling under the weight of my torso; I sensed disaster approaching. I looked down cautiously at the scales, only to see the needle fixed firmly on the fifteen stone mark. There I was, a sixteen year old teenager weighing almost as much as my age. All of the meat and potato pies I had eaten in my youth suddenly flashed before my eyes. I was officially too fat to join the Royal Navy!

I stood back off the scales and started to get dressed. I had the same feeling you get when you are halfway through your driving test and you carry out a manoeuvre that you know only too well has caused you to fail. In the corner of my eye I could see the doctor writing down a brief assessment on his marking sheet with his spectacles balancing precariously on the edge of his nose – he didn't look impressed.

Within five minutes I was walking out of the surgery feeling extremely de-jected. He had informed me that I needed to lose a stone in weight before they would permit me to start the training course. On the way out of the surgery he had also handed me a small sheet of paper which detailed what I should and should not eat if I was to be successful in transforming myself from a fat spotty teenager to the kind of young man the Royal Navy would permit through its doors.

Whilst I sat at the bus stop waiting for the bus to take me home I started to study the diet sheet the doctor had handed me. Even my pet rabbit could not survive on this crap, I thought to myself! The sheet of paper consisted of the following recommended meal:

Breakfast - scrambled eggs on two slices of toast with one cup of tea.

Mid-morning snack – one apple

Lunch – one jacket potato with small portion of beans

Afternoon snack – one banana

Evening meal – one small portion of chicken breast, half a cup of boiled rice and vegetables

Evening snack – one wholemeal biscuit and a small glass of milk

(Note – drink one pint of water twenty minutes before each meal)

Now for most people, this would seem to be a decent daily intake of food; however, it was probably half of what I would normally eat, which explains why I was overweight.

The reason I am talking about this now is that I have learnt throughout my life that if I apply discipline and structure to my work I **WILL** be successful. Discipline is the root cause of my success. If you are disciplined and determined when writing and publishing your book you **will** be successful. Here's what happened next.

As the bus approached to take me home from the medical I made a decision. This decision proved to be the catalyst that changed not only my approach to fitness but also my entire attitude to life. I decided there and then that I would walk home instead of getting the bus. As I walked home I promised myself that I would walk to college every day and then back home again. As I began walking briskly my heart beat increased and I began to feel more positive and enthusiastic about the future. It only took me 4 weeks to lose the weight required, and it was from that point on that I realised that if I applied myself and worked hard, success would follow.

The Royal Navy was a fantastic experience for me as it gave me responsibility, a trade, a sense of purpose and, most importantly, discipline. I will talk about discipline as I progress through this guide, as it is something you are going to have to take notice of when you start to write and publish your first book. Basically, from the age of 16 I was 'required' to conduct myself in a disciplined manner, and this is something that I carried over into my next career as a firefighter and then as an author – discipline is one of the main reasons for my success, and it will also be one of yours, too.

After serving just 4 years in the Royal Navy I decided to follow in the footsteps of my father Tony and join the Fire Service. At the age of 21 I applied to join Kent Fire Brigade, and on January the 25th 1993 I started a job that would turn out to be a successful 17-year career in the Fire Service. Whilst in the Fire Service I worked hard, sat my promotional exams, and soon found opportunities came my way. One of the very first mentors I had in life was a man called Mick Brooker – he was my officer-in-charge whilst serving as a firefighter at Maidstone Fire Station, and he would often give me 'opportunities' to develop and grow as an individual. He would insist that I gave weekly lectures and presentations to the rest of the Watch at the Fire Station on subjects that focused on firefighter operational procedures. Although I didn't realise it at the time, all of this experience was setting me up to become one of the UK's most successful authors.

After a couple of years working under Mick at Maidstone Fire Station I managed to secure a temporary promotion at the Training Centre. Mick had been impressed at the standard of my presentations and decided to put me forward for a Leading Firefighter Instructors position at the County Training Centre. I loved every minute of this job, and I actually ended up spending 4 years in this post teaching people how to join the Fire Service and running my own firefighter recruit training courses. Once again, although I didn't realise it at the time my future as an author and publisher was starting to take shape.

HOW DOES ALL THIS AFFECT YOU?

Many of you will be reading this and wondering what the heck it has got to do with being an author and publisher. Well, apart from the discipline required to become a successful author you also need to have an idea for the book that you intend writing. Most of us have lots of experience in life which we can tap into and use when researching ideas for writing books. Whether it's by way of our qualifications, our career, hobbies and interests, or our passions, we all have something to write about. During the next chapter I will go into researching ideas for book subjects in more detail, but basically my first book idea focused on what I was good at, and that was teaching people how to get a job in the Fire Service.

After leaving the Training Centre I then started to rise through the ranks of the Fire Service, and I eventually ended up in charge of a District under the title of Assistant Divisional Officer. My salary at the time was in excess of £55,000 per year and I was also handed a new company car every 3 years and one of the best pension's available. Despite all of this, I was unhappy. Having spoken to many aspiring authors over the years, many of them often tell me about their frustrations in their job and how they do not find it fulfilling – I felt exactly the same when working in the Fire Service. Although it was a secure career and very well paid I did not enjoy the last 5 years or so of my career, simply because it wasn't *creative* enough for me. As an author you will undoubtedly have a need and desire to be *creative* – it is what drives us forward and is also what keeps us happy as individuals. I did not realise I had this need until I started to write my first book.

Since that day when I sat down in my cellar to write my first book, I have gone on to author and publish over 150 books, many of which have become best-sellers. More importantly, I have been very happy in my work as an author and publisher, and I have absolutely no regrets about leaving the Fire Service. Like I said, my first book idea came from a niche I spotted whilst working in the Fire Service, and as I explain how this unfolded I want you to also think about the different experiences you have had in life so far and how they might be used in order to write your first book.

As I progressed through my career in the Fire Service many people used to approach me and ask me for advice on how to get a job as a firefighter. I would often invite them around to my house for an hour or so and set about teaching them how to prepare for the firefighter selection process, usually in exchange for a crate of my favourite beer! More often than not, those people that I taught would pass the selection process and end up getting a career as a firefighter.

As time went on I can remember thinking to myself that there must be a way for me to turn this level of expertise I had into a business. I started to carry out some research on the internet to see what information was available to help people to join the Fire Service. After a few minutes of research I found the level of information to be limited, and this was my opportunity to change my life and create a successful business out of my expertise. For some reason I decided to call my publishing business 'how2become', and I sat down to write my first book in the cellar of my house on my old crappy Hewlett Packard computer. Despite having no previous 'writing' experience, I was determined to be successful.

My first guide took me approximately 3 months to complete, and I started selling it via my website how2become.com. I attended an internet business start-up course with my good friend Simon Coulson to learn how to set up a website and direct traffic to it. After a few months' hard work and perseverance I started to sell my guide to customers throughout the UK. Although things were slow to begin with, it wasn't long before I was selling 30 copies every day of the week! As you can imagine, this was a very exciting time for me as I could sense there was large gap in the market that needed to be filled – and it was my intention to fill it as fast as I could.

My first guide on getting into the Fire Service was selling so well that I was filling up three post boxes every day. At this point I was still working in the Fire Service, and I often found myself working until 3am writing, researching and packing the orders which were being received via my website. At this point in time I hadn't even considered Amazon as an option for selling my guide. I sat down and constructed a business plan, and then decided that my next book would need to be on getting a job in the Royal Navy. After all, I had experience of passing the selection process so it made perfect sense to write a book on this subject, as I knew there was demand.

After completing my second book (How to join the Royal Navy) I realised that I had now run out of ideas, yet I still had this burning desire to grow my publishing business and increase the number of books in my 'how2become' range. I had identified, through carrying out key research which I will disclose in the next chapter, that there was huge demand for information on getting careers such as train driver, prison officer, cabin crew and probation officer. I figured that the only way I could get the 'insider' information I needed to write my books was to actually go through the selection process myself – and that's exactly what I did!

I sat down in my cellar and began filling out application forms for all of these jobs. When I received a letter inviting me along to the assessment centre, I would prepare thoroughly for it. After passing the assessment centre I would then attend the interview and do my utmost to pass it. At the end of the interview I would return to my car and immediately write down all of the questions I was asked, so that I could use these within the books I was writing.

More often than not I would be offered the job. However, if I was unsuccessful, I would write off and seek feedback on my performance which again would help me to write great content for my books. This would allow me to use the information received from the employer to help other people perform better when they attended the assessment centre or interview. Although I did not realise it at the time, I was slowly becoming an 'expert' at passing job selection processes, whilst at the same time adding to my list of interview questions, sample tests and insider knowledge on how to get specialist careers.

During the years that followed I carried on writing my books and growing my publishing business, using the same formula time and time again. It is that exact same formula that I will teach you within this book, and I feel very confident you are going to find it a very useful tool in your writing and publishing armoury.

The information I have just provided you with is a very brief snapshot of how I fell into writing and publishing, and the steps I have taken to gain sufficient knowledge to write my books. It is designed to give you the confidence that despite not having any prior writing or publishing experience you can become a best-selling author, publish your own book(s), and keep all of the profits in the process. During the next few chapters I will go into detail about the processes I use to write and publish my books.

CHAPTER 2

MY TOP 10 TIPS FOR WRITING AND PUBLISHING SUCCESS

Get instant access to over 32 hours' worth of online training videos and support at:

www.BookPublishingAcademy.co.uk

MY TOP 10 TIPS FOR WRITING AND PUBLISHING SUCCESS

Within this chapter of the book I have decided to list a number of insider tips and advice that will help you to achieve success when both writing and publishing books. These tips have helped me to continually achieve success in my publishing business, and I would like to share them with you. Although some of them may appear to be common-sense, please take the time to read them and implement them during your writing and publishing strategy.

TIP 1 – DO NOT GET A BOOK PUBLISHING DEAL UNLESS YOU ARE THE NEXT JK ROWLING

Perhaps the main reason you are reading this book is because you are serious about publishing your own book yourself. This is great news! I can safely say that I am qualified to advise you here, simply because I have actually had a book publishing deal myself before I started self-publishing. In fact, I had a six book publishing deal. One of the main reasons why I got myself the publishing deals was to learn the entire book publishing process myself. Of course, I did not disclose this to the publisher at the time, but it was my intention to learn the whole book publishing process so that I could do it myself and keep all of the profits in the process.

I can remember sitting in the plush London offices of the publishing company that I was trying to get a publishing contract with. They were very professional and explained the entire process to me in detail. After reading my manuscripts they informed me that they would need to get approval from their company Director before the six draft publishing contracts would be sent over to me for consideration. At this point it was also explained to me the royalty rate I would receive from each book sold. After some tough negotiations I managed to get myself 15% of net profits per book that was sold. To put it in simple terms, this effectively meant I would get approximately 30-50 pence for every book that was sold. Now, call me ungrateful, but this did not sound fair at all. I was expected to write the content (60,000 words per book), and in exchange I would receive a royalty of just 15% of net profits for printed book sales. On the train home I considered the offer carefully and managed to persuade myself that the contracts were worth more to me than the royalty rate simply because I would get to learn the entire publishing process, which would eventually mean that I could do it myself. And that's exactly what I did.

Here are the pros and cons of getting a standard book publishing deal:

Pros

- You do not have to put up any money in order to get your book published
- The publisher **might** invest some money to promote your book
- Your book **might** get stocked in Waterstones stores and WHSmith, although there are no guarantees
- You will usually receive an advance of royalties

Cons

- You will generally get a very low royalty rate (approx. 10% - 15% of net profits)
- You may lose the rights to the work
- You will be tied in to a contract for a very long time, effectively meaning you cannot sell your book anywhere else
- You will lose control of the book cover design, title and the branding
- As and when required you will have to provide updates of your book to the publisher
- The advance that you receive is exactly that, an advance. It will need to be earned against any royalties your book generates, meaning you may never see a royalty cheque
- The publishing contract can take a long time to get agreed, and negotiations can often be very frustrating. It took me a year to get approval for my book publishing contracts

Hopefully you can now see the reasons why I encourage you to not get a book publishing deal, unless you are the next JK Rowling of course.

TIP 2 – DON'T BE IN IT FOR THE MONEY

Of course, most people write and publish a book to make money; I fully appreciate that. However, whilst the financial reward can be amazing I advise that you put any ideas of financial reward to the back of your mind for the time being. The reason for this can be summed up in the following paragraph:

"When you write your first book, concentrate on writing chapters which your readers will find useful, enjoyable and impossible to put down. If you do this, the financial reward will come regardless."

Most people ask me how long it will take them to see a 5-figure monthly return from their writing efforts. My answer to this question is simple – if you focus solely on the financial return then you probably won't see any profits at all. I then encourage them to focus on writing great content that will be of benefit to the reader, as this will have the following effect:

1. The reader will love the book, and they will then be more likely to leave a positive review on Amazon. If they do this the book will sell more copies.

2. The more genuine 'verified' reviews your books receives, the better chance it will have of selling. If you write poor quality content your book will almost definitely get criticised online.

3. Your readers will want to buy more of your books if the first one is great. This will also have the added benefit of giving your motivational levels a boost, something which is crucial to us as authors.

4. If you write great content then the chance of upselling in your book will greatly increase. For example, within my 'How2become a firefighter' book I promote 1-day training courses on how to get into the Fire Service. I can easily get 20 people to attend each course, all of which have decided to purchase and attend my course after reading my book.

TIP 3 – HOW MANY PAGES SHOULD I WRITE?

Another common question I get asked is how many pages should my book be? This is a very difficult question to answer, as the answer will be very much dependent on the genre/subject of the book and also the type of reader and their needs. It will also depend on the pricing structure of the book, something which I will explain in greater detail during the next tip. To give you an idea of how I would decide on how many pages my book should be, take a look at the following case study:

Sample book writing case study – Michael Watson

Michael Watson is an author who I coached to write his first book through my coaching programme. After spending time with Michael it became apparent that he was working as a social worker, providing expert advice to parents who were going through the family court process. He wanted to find an alternative way to generate extra income for himself, so I encouraged him to write a book entitled **'How to represent yourself in Family Court'**. I believed this was a good book subject title for Michael to write because of the following reasons:

1. Michael was an expert in this field, therefore the book would be easier to sell because he had instant **authority.**

2. At the time of writing austerity measures had taken a hold on society, and there was not much Legal Aid to help parents go through the Family Court process. As a result there was more demand for his expertise.

3. The divorce rate at the time of writing was still on the increase. This fact led me to believe there would be demand for his book for many years to come.

4. After carrying out effective research I was positive that this book would sell.

One of the first things Michael asked me was how long his book should be. I explained to him that the type of person likely to read the book would not have the time or desire to sit down and spend hours reading technical or over-complicated content. I also explained that they would probably be emotionally upset and would not have the energy to read a 'thick' book. I also went onto explain that there was an opportunity within his book to upsell by way of offering his readers one-to-one coaching, via Skype or in person, or even the opportunity to attend a 1-day training course with Michael. I then concluded that the book should be no longer than 100 pages in length, and it should also be a size that could easily fit in someone's back pocket or handbag.

TIP 4 – HOW MUCH SHOULD I SELL MY BOOK FOR?

This is a very good question, which I will answer during this tip. The bottom line is this; if you price your book too cheaply you won't make much money. On the other hand, if you price it too steep you could put off potential customers. There are obviously higher production costs associated with physical books, whereas eBooks and Kindle books will give you financial reward far quicker.

Before you decide how much to price your book, consider the following points:

1. Amazon will take up to 60% of the recommended retail price (RRP) of your printed book, depending on which programme you decide to sell your book through (more on this later during the relevant Amazon chapters). Understandably, most people are immediately put off by this, however please read my Amazon chapters before dismissing Amazon as a marketplace to sell your work.

2. When you sell your book through the Amazon Kindle programme you will be able to choose either a 70% or 35% royalty rate, depending on what price you decide to sell your book at. The level of royalty you choose will be mostly profit, as you will have no delivery or ongoing production costs.

3. With printed books you will have to get them printed yourself, unless you decide to opt for the **Amazon Createspace** programme. I choose to get my books printed through a 3rd party printer and this method works very well for me, simply because I want to sell via multiple-channels and not just on Amazon. If I did want to sell solely on Amazon then I would probably choose the Createspace programme to reduce my costs.

4. The **unit price** per printed book will very much depend on the printer you use. There are lots of printing companies out there vying for your business – the more you spend with them, the less it will cost you per book to get printed. Personally, I pay between £1 and £1.50 per 100 pages, but I do spend in excess of £100,000 per year with my chosen printer.

The vast majority of books I sell will be launched with a RRP of between £13 and £15. I very rarely sell my books for less than this, simply because I aim to make at least £5 clear profit per book that I sell. For the books that I sell on my own website I do not have to give Amazon, or anyone else for that matter, the 60% margin, and therefore I will make a lot more profit per book sold via this marketplace. Because of this it is within my interests to sell as many copies as I can via my own website. At the time of writing I take in excess of 100 trans-actions per day via my website.

The selling price will also be very much dependent on the genre of the book. For example, within my careers niche I can realistically ask £13 - £15 per book because the reader, if successful in landing a job after using my book, will probably receive a salary of up to £30,000 per year, therefore a £13 - £15 investment is a reasonable exchange. However, if you are selling a novel or fiction printed book then you may need to lower your price to the £10 mark or slightly lower. If it is a Kindle version, your price point will be lower still.

Before you decide how much to price your book at, ask yourself the following questions:

1. How much will it cost me to get my physical book printed?

2. How much profit will I be left with per printed book after costs?

3. What price point are other people within my genre selling their books at? (This is a great strategy to use when considering the price of your book)

4. What price would I personally be willing to pay for a book of the same standard?

Having answered all of the above questions and taken into consideration all of the additional advice within this tip, you should be able to come up with a suitable recommended retail price for you book. Whatever happens, once you list your book at the RRP you can always reduce it later on if you find it is not selling. Alternatively, you can always increase your prices if you feel it is too cheap.

TIP 5 – SERIOUSLY CONSIDER PUBLISHING A PRINTED BOOK

Most authors I speak to believe the sale of printed books is on the decline – this is simply not true. Although the sale of Kindle books is now outstripping that of printed books on Amazon, the sale of printed books is still on the increase. Whether this trend continues in to the future remains to be seen; however, within certain niches I believe there will always be a strong demand for printed books. Whether or not you decide to opt for a printed book will very much depend on the genre of your book, and also the budget you have at your disposal.

If you are writing and self-publishing a fiction novel or mystery, crime and thriller book then I would advise you start off with a Kindle version. These genres of book tend to sell well in this format simply because people like to read them whilst travelling on the train, plane or whilst on holiday. If you intend publishing a book in either careers, business, finance, law, self-help, motivational, property, or business start-up then you should seriously consider printed books, as they tend to sell better in this format. To give you an example, many of my printed books sell 5 times as many copies as they do on Kindle! This is not surprising, as most of my books are manuals which require a need to try out sample test questions; something which cannot be done with a Kindle.

Graph demonstrating Kindle sales vs. Physical (printed) book sales on Amazon

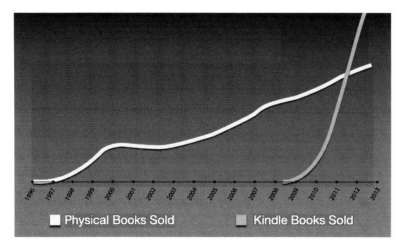

There are lots of benefits to publishing books on Kindle. Here they are:
- Relatively cheap to get published
- Quick to publish on the Amazon Digital Text Platform (DTP)
- High royalty rate (70% or 35%, depending on the pricing of your book)
- Huge demand for Kindle books in certain genres

There are also a few downsides to publishing books on Kindle, too. Here they are:
- Easier for customers to ask for a refund. The refund rate for Kindle books is higher than that of printed books
- The perceived value of a Kindle book is lower than a printed book
- A Kindle book will not reach places that a printed book can reach, and therefore the chance to upsell might be limited to just one reader

And here are the benefits to publishing books in Printed format:
- There are still many people who like the 'touch, feel and smell' of a printed book

- A printed book is more likely to get passed around other readers, therefore increasing the opportunity for you to upsell to a wider audience. For example, I do know that most of my printed books are being used in schools and universities up and down the UK. This is great FREE promotion for my brand.

- For people running a business a printed book is now seen as the 'new business card'. Read the chapter entitled 'Books for Business Owners' to find out exactly what I mean.

- As a published author there is far more prestige attached to having your work published in physical/printed format.

- Printed books are a fantastic promotional tool when trying to upsell or promote additional products or services.

So, the choice of whether or not to publish your book in printed format is entirely down to you, your needs, and your budget.

TIP 6 – GET YOUR BOOK COVER DESIGN WRONG AND YOU WILL NOT SELL ANY BOOKS, REGARDLESS OF HOW GOOD THE CONTENT IS!

It doesn't seem that long ago that we were all buying our books in High Street stores such as Waterstones. The first thing we are hit with when we enter a

High Street book store is the mass of book spines sitting neatly on the book shelves. The book spine design and presentation was far more important pre-Amazon days. An example of this is the 'Dummies Guides'. The next time you go into a Waterstones branch take a look at all the brightly coloured spines on the shelves representing the many Dummies guides on sale. The high florescent colouring of their spines was an example of very clever marketing in my opinion, simply because our eyes are drawn more to this colour than others. The Dummies guides design does a fantastic job of grabbing our attention.

Things have now changed, and we are buying more and more books online through stores such as Amazon and the Book Depository. Therefore, because of how books are presented online the book spine no longer has any significance during the buying process. What does have more significance is the actual front book cover itself – get this bit wrong and you will not sell any books, regardless of how good the content is. During a later chapter of this book I have dedicated an entire section to creating quality book cover designs and the kind of things I will consider when hiring a book cover designer. Read the chapter carefully and follow the tips and guidance contained within it to create truly awesome book cover designs that will ensure your books sell.

TIP 7 – WORK HARD, PERSEVERE AND DON'T GIVE UP!

When you sit down to write your first book it is understandably going to take up a lot of your time. Your evenings, weekends and every other spare minute will be needed to get your book completed, but the hard work and determination will be worth it.

When writing your book you will understandably find yourself, on occasions, feeling de-motivated and lacking the desire to write. When this happens stop writing and take a break. I have learnt over the years to only write when I feel that I want to. Whilst I am no procrastinator, which is probably due to my military background, I do sometimes find it hard to write content. I have learnt not to get down or de-motivated about the situation, and instead I simply take a few days off and come back to it when I am ready to.

It is very easy to burn yourself out as an author, and you will need to plan ahead to avoid this happening. This is why I encourage new authors and self-publishers to have a mentor – a mentor will be able to guide you and offer those all-important words of encouragement when they are most needed.

When writing and publishing your book you will need to have plenty of energy, so make sure you get adequate rest and exercise and that you eat a healthy diet. You will no doubt have heard of the saying 'Work hard, play hard'. Most successful authors and publishers know how to create a healthy work/lifestyle balance, and this is something that you should try to incorporate into your action plan very early on. Take time out to do things you like doing, and reward yourself when you reach significant milestones or chapters.

Finally, like most people I enjoy a few beers at weekends. However, I find that I am at my most productive when I cut out alcohol altogether. I have also noticed that when I cut out alcohol my turnover and profits actually increase, simply because I get more done! When writing your book(s) I would urge you to consider your diet and alcohol intake – we need you to have as much energy as possible when starting out, and all of these considerations will help.

Learn to take responsibility

Remember that you are the key to your destiny. You control your future and therefore you must take responsibility for it. In order to become a successful author and self-publisher you don't have to be good at everything. Concentrate on coming up with book ideas and writing them; outsource everything else. I understand that in order to become successful I will need to hire people who are better than me at specific jobs or tasks – hence my love for outsourcing, which I will cover in greater detail during a later chapter.

TIP 8 – WORK TO AN ACTION PLAN

Another reason for my success is the fact that I work to a strict action plan. When I write a book I always use the exact same action plan, which will consist of action points such as:

- How many pages I will write everyday

- The type of research I will carry out

- The proposed chapters of the book

- When I intend ordering the book cover artwork

- The date I will put the book on Amazon 'pre-order'

I get asked a lot questions about how long it generally takes me to write a book. This very much depends on my enthusiasm levels, how excited I am about the book I am writing, and also whether or not the book is seasonal.

What I mean by this is whether the book needs to be published and on sale for the busiest time of year for the book subject. For example, if you are writing fiction or a novel then these books tend to sell very well in the build up to Christmas and during the school holidays. My career books always sell very well in January, when people are generally looking to make changes to their lives as a whole.

Despite still typing with only two fingers, I managed to complete the first draft manuscript for this particular book within 17 days. I felt very excited about writing this book, and I found putting the content together quite easy because I know my subject inside out. Other times it can take me longer, but generally if I stick to my action plan I can write a book relatively quickly.

Let's assume you want to write a book which will consist of 100 pages. Within your action plan I would recommend you set out a minimum number of pages to write every day of the week. If you set out to write three pages every day then you will have almost completed the book within a month. Writing three pages per day is something you can achieve, for sure!

TIP 9 – ENTER YOUR BOOK INTO AWARDS

Entering your book or publishing business into business awards can have a massive impact on the number of books you sell. Apart from receiving free/ invaluable publicity for your book, the recognition itself will drive you on to write more books.

To date I have entered my publishing business into four different business awards. The first business awards I entered was the HSBC Bank Start-Up Stars Awards. As part of the entry process I was required to complete a short questionnaire which asked me specific questions about my business and the books I was writing. Just by submitting the application form to enter the awards made me look at my business and business strategy in a different light. In order to give my business a better chance of winning I decided to make some major improvements to my strategy. To my surprise I actually won the HSBC Start-Up Stars South East region award, which then meant I went through to the national final at the Savoy Hotel in London. Although I did not win the final, I was voted as one of the best new businesses in the UK. Not bad for a firefighter with no previous experience running his book publishing business from his cellar! The publicity I received following this award was amazing. I appeared in local and national newspapers, and it really gave my 'brand' a tremendous boost. It also drove me on to write more books.

After being shortlisted the following year in the National Online Recruitment Awards I then decided to enter awards specifically targeted at book publishers. I joined the Independent Publishing Guild and entered their awards during the same year. Once again, by entering the awards it made me focus on making improvements to my business. In 2012 and 2013 I was shortlisted in the Publisher of the Year category as Best Newcomer. This is what the judges said about my business:

> *"How2Become is shortlisted on the back of rising print sales, down-loads and web visits since launching. Judges admired the company's achievement on limited resources and its testimonials from grateful readers. "How2Become has performed well with decent margins — and is helping people to get jobs in difficult times."*

From the above comments made by the judges two words really stood out for me – **"helping people"**. At the start of this book I explained to you how, when writing books, I will always focus on writing high-quality content that is of benefit to the reader. These two words written by the judges just go to reaffirm this strategy – if you help people, the rewards will follow.

Finally, in 2014 I was once again shortlisted in the National Publishing Awards, this time in the 'Worldwide Specialist Consumer of the Year' category.

At the back of the book I have provided a useful resources section which lists the book awards you may want to enter once you have published your book.

TIP 10 – USE OUTSOURCERS

Some of the judges' comments that I made reference to in the previous tip were in relation to my achievements on "limited resources." What they basically meant was the fact that I have achieved so much without employing lots of people. At the time of writing I employ just one member of staff for four hours per day. The reason why I am able to do this is because I make good use of outsourcers.

Outsourcing is the practise of hiring others to carry out work that you are either not good at or that you don't have the time to do. Or, my preferred description of outsourcing is this:

To obtain a professional service from an external expert in order to MASSIVELY increase the profits in your business

I consistently generate six-figure net profits every year, and this is largely because I outsource effectively.

When people start a business they generally find themselves doing everything. This was certainly the case for me when I first started out. I can remember doing literally **EVERYTHING** in the beginning such as answering the customer service emails, learning how to build the website from which I was going to sell my books, writing my books, and also sending out the books to my customers. As time went on I learnt more about the art of outsourcing and how it could free up more time for me to work 'on' my publishing business as opposed to working 'in' it.

I generally work on the 80/20 principle, which effectively means that in my life there are certain activities that I do (my 20%) which account for the majority (my 80%) of my happiness and my output. My 20% consists of the following:

- I keep fit.
- I eat healthily.
- I only DO things that I am good at (write books and mentor authors)

I then outsource the rest!

My advice to you as an aspiring author is to only work on the things you are good at, and that will probably only mean writing the content for your books. For example, it is very important for my publishing business (How2become. com) that I actually *write* the books and present the online training videos. After all, it is my skill and expertise in recruitment that people are paying for, therefore it would not make sense if I outsourced these elements of the business. I also actually really enjoy writing books, too. Here's a full list of things that I outsource in my publishing business:

- I outsource my website design/development
- I outsource my book cover design and branding
- I outsource my proofreading/editing
- I outsource my typesetting (preparing the manuscript for print)
- I outsource my printing
- I outsource my customer service/care
- I outsource my eBook conversion

- I outsource my website sales-copy
- I outsource my advertising/marketing strategy

Before you employ someone in any business you should ask yourself the following questions:

Q1. Do I really need to employ this person?

Q2. Are there alternatives, such as using outsourcers?

If you can outsource the work then I would strongly encourage you to do so.

During one of the later chapters I will go into more detail about the art of outsourcing and how it will help you to self-publish your book(s).

CHAPTER 3
RESEARCHING IDEAS FOR BOOK SUBJECTS

Get instant access to over 32 hours' worth of online training videos and support at:

www.BookPublishingAcademy.co.uk

RESEARCHING IDEAS FOR BOOK SUBJECTS

This has to be the most important aspect of my publishing strategy. By carrying out effective research I am able to pretty much determine whether or not a book will become a success, even before I have started writing it. Most authors understandably start writing their book without carrying out any research in order to ascertain whether or not it has a chance of selling. I believe this is a big mistake. If you carry out little or no research prior to writing your book then you will soon become de-motivated once you realise it doesn't sell as many copies as you hoped it would. This will then have the knock-on effect of draining all of the drive and enthusiasm which is needed to write further books.

To help you get off to the right start with any book writing venture, take a look at the following important steps.

STEP 1 – CHOOSING A GENRE

The first step in writing your book is to select a genre. Whilst there are many different book genres out there, I recommend you choose one which:

- you are passionate about;
- you have a desire to write in;
- you have knowledge or expertise of;
- there is demand.

I recommend you choose your genre from the list of categories listed on Amazon, purely because I can safely say this is the place you will sell the vast majority of your books – more about Amazon in later chapters.

At the time of writing, the following book categories are listed on Amazon:

• Art, Architecture & Photography

• Audiobooks

• Biography

• Books for University

• Business, Finance & Law

• Calendars, Diaries, Annuals & More

• Children's Books

• Comics & Graphic Novels

- Computing & Internet
- Crime, Thrillers & Mystery
- eBooks
- Fiction
- Food & Drink
- Foreign Language
- Gay & Lesbian
- Health, Family & Lifestyle
- History
- Home & Garden
- Horror
- Humour
- Languages (Learning)
- Mind, Body & Spirit
- Music, Stage & Screen
- Poetry, Drama & Criticism
- Reference
- Religion & Spirituality
- Romance
- School Books
- Science & Nature
- Science Fiction & Fantasy
- Scientific, Technical & Medical
- Society, Politics & Philosophy
- Sports, Hobbies & Games
- Travel & Holiday

Believe it or not, my 'how2become' career books fall under the 'Business, Finance and Law' category on Amazon.

Which is the biggest genre?

Unsurprisingly, of the people who buy at least one book a year 8 out of 10 buy a fiction book. The best-selling fiction books are mystery, crime and thriller. Now, I am not saying that you should go away and start writing a book in the fiction category, far from it. What I am saying, though, is that it is worth carrying out some research on the level of demand that your chosen genre falls into.

My niche 'career books' genre is actually a very small market with regards to demand, yet I have still managed to make over £3,000,000 from it so far. On the flipside, Erotic Fiction is one of the largest book markets on Amazon, yet it is discreetly hidden from the homepage. When you get time, type in 'erotic fiction' into the Amazon search bar on the homepage and take a look at the rankings of some of the books in this category!

Applying Maslow's Hierarchy of Needs to book research

During my research I will more often than not use Maslow's Hierarchy of Needs. Maslow wanted to understand what motivates people. He believed that individuals possess a set of motivation systems unrelated to rewards or unconscious desires. Maslow stated that people are motivated to achieve certain needs. When one need is fulfilled a person seeks to fulfil the next one, and so on. When I think of a potential book subject I will always ask myself the following question - "is there demand for my book based on Maslow's triangle of needs?" Although this method of research does not guarantee a book will sell, it does give me the confidence that my book has a better chance of selling as it falls into a category which defines the basic requirement of people's everyday needs.

To demonstrate how effective Maslow's triangle is, Facebook sits slap bang in the **'LOVE AND BELONGING'** section of the triangle. Many people have been surprised at the success of Facebook, however if we study Maslow's Hierarchy of Needs we can see that a 'sense of connection' is a must to ALL human beings. This is exactly the reason why we feel a sense of connection when people click 'LIKE' on a photograph we have posted on our Facebook page.

In order to explain the process that I follow better I have listed which genre of books fall into which level of Maslow's triangle.

Maslow's Hierarchy of Needs

So, once you have chosen the genre or title for your book take a quick look at Maslow's triangle to see whether or not it fits into one or more of the Maslow needs.

Of course, there are many authors out there reading this book who will already have an idea for a book subject. For those of you who are in this position, I still recommend you carry out the **researching steps** within this chapter in order to ascertain whether or not your book will sell.

STEP 2 – CHOOSING A BOOK SUBJECT IDEA

Once you have chosen your book genre it is now time to choose the actual **subject** for your book.

One of the most effective ways to choose a book subject is to use my BOOK IDEAS GENERATION FORM. The form was created a few years ago when I noticed a pattern to ideas I was generating. The form is shown on the next page and is immediately followed by an explanation for each section of the form. I recommend you start completing the form as this will help you to choose a book subject idea.

Richard McMunn's Book Ideas Generation Form

QUESTIONS	ANSWERS	BOOK IDEA
What qualifications do I have?		
What am I good at?		
What courses have I been on during my life?		
Have people ever asked me for help or advice?		
What am I passionate about?		
Have I ever won any awards?		
What do my friends or relatives know that could help me?		

I have used this form to great effect over the last few years in order to generate book ideas, and I am certain it will help you too. I have also used it on numerous occasions to help my students come up with book ideas via my one-to-one coaching programme.

For example, an author called David Isaacs approached me in 2010 asking for help on writing and publishing a book. I asked him to complete the form, and it transpired that he held a Masters qualification in mathematics. I coached David to write and publish a book entitled 'GCSE Mathematics Questions and Answers', which subsequently went on to become a number **1 best-seller** on Amazon – proof that the form really does work!

To demonstrate how I have used the form over the years, I will provide you with my answers to the questions and also the book ideas I generated from those answers.

QUESTIONS	ANSWERS	BOOK IDEA
What qualifications do I have?	3 x GCSE's	How to become a millionaire with poor exam qualifications!
What am I good at?	Helping others	My 'how2become' series of books
What courses have I been on during my life?	Health and Safety courses during my time in the Fire Service	How to carry out a Fire Risk Assessment on your property
Have people ever asked me for help or advice?	How to join the Fire Service How to write a book	My 'how2become a firefighter' book This book!
What am I passionate about?	Helping others to achieve success	This book and all of my 'how2become' books
Have I ever won any awards?	Numerous business awards	How to become an Award Winning business
What do my friends or relatives know that could help me?	My father was a magistrate	How2become a magistrate

You will notice from my answers that I will never be short of book ideas. One question which should open lots of doors for you in terms of book subject ideas is the final one – "What do my friends or relatives know that could help me?" When completing the form, it dawned on me that my Father was a magistrate and that he was a source of information I could potentially tap into in order to help me to write a book on this subject. Whilst he would not disclose any information regarding how to pass the selection process, he was able to tell me key facts about the role and the type of qualities and attributes needed to become a competent magistrate – after using his information and carrying out further research I created a best-selling book entitled 'How to become a magistrate' which has made thousands of pounds on Amazon and through Waterstones.

Using the newspapers to generate niche book ideas

Newspapers are a great source of information for identifying niche book ideas. A few times a week I will spend at least 30 minutes in my local Costa Coffee reading the papers and searching for ideas from which to write new books. Here's an example of a book idea I spotted in **The Telegraph** one day:

HEADLINE: British Airways to recruit 800 pilots

The Telegraph

Home News World Sport Finance Comment Culture Travel Life Women Fashion

Companies Comment Personal Finance Economics Markets Festival of Business Hot 1000

HOME » FINANCE » NEWS BY SECTOR » TRANSPORT

British Airways to recruit 800 pilots

British Airways is turning to YouTube to boost its biggest pilot recruitment campaign.

Half of the 800 new pilots will come through the British Airways Future Pilot Programme.

By David Millward, Transport Editor
5:45AM BST 11 Aug 2011

48 Comments

Transport
Travel News »
Finance »
News by Sector »
Business Latest News »
David Millward »

In Finance »

Axe carbon tax to keep lights on and cut bills

'Boris island may be dumped by Davies'

As soon as I saw this headline, I knew it was a great opportunity to write a book entitled 'How to become an airline pilot'. If British Airways needed to recruit 800 pilots then the competition for these jobs would be huge! I also figured that if British Airways needed to recruit that many pilots, other airlines would probably soon follow suit. There was just one problem; I had absolutely no idea how to become a pilot!

Using my 'can-do' attitude I sat there in the coffee shop thinking of ways I could find an airline pilot to either help me to write the book or write it for me with a view to sharing the royalties. After a few minutes searching online I found a forum for pilots entitled pprune.org. I then registered as a user and simply posted a message on their forum asking if there were any pilots available to help me write a book on this subject. Soon after posting the message I had found myself a pilot and we arranged to meet up to discuss how he could help me to write the book. Again, this book ended up becoming a best-seller on Amazon. I can spot book niche ideas every single day of the week, and I can confidently say that I will never run out of ideas – the only problem is having enough time in the day to write them all.

Once you follow my methods and strategies for generating exciting and niche book ideas I can assure that you will never run out of them.

What is HOT right now?

Another way to generate book ideas is to look out for book subjects which are selling really well right now. For example, a few years back '50 SHADES OF GREY' burst onto the scene, making the author an overnight millionaire and book publishing sensation. Whilst I have never read this book, I have heard that the standard of writing is not that great. What was particularly great about this book was the manner in which it was marketed. The publisher who launched the book clearly knew what they were doing as they tapped into a genre which most people would not admit to enjoying reading – erotic fiction.

You will recall earlier that I mentioned how this market is absolutely huge on Amazon, yet Amazon does not make a song and dance about it, primarily to protect its family friendly image. For those people like myself who like to keep an eye on the publishing world it was no surprise when immediately following the launch of this book other authors decided to write their own version of this book. Whilst these authors were not copying an idea, they were clever in the fact that they were tapping into a genre which was really HOT at the time.

As an author you should keep your eyes wide open for opportunities which spring up on a regular basis. If you see an opportunity, consider writing a book on the subject.

Book subjects to avoid

Whilst there is a market out there for most book subjects, you do need to be careful not to fall into the trap of writing a book where either the competition is so fierce or where the market is over-saturated. Through trial and error I have learnt over the years that books will sell far better if they are targeted towards a particular niche section of individuals or groups. Don't just assume that because there is big demand for a particular subject that your book will sell thousands of copies – consider niche areas of your chosen book first as these are far more likely to sell better and provide you with a sustainable future as an author. An example of this would be in relation to a fitness book. There are so many books available on fitness that you would be hard pushed to ever make any money at all from a book that simply covers 'general' fitness. However, if you choose a niche area of the fitness genre, fitness for pregnant women for example, it will have a better chance of selling.

STEP 3 – HOW MANY PEOPLE ARE SEARCHING FOR YOUR BOOK SUBJECT ONLINE?

Once you have come up with your book subject idea, you now need to take the time to see whether or not there is a market for it. In order to achieve this I recommend you use the GOOGLE KEYWORD PLANNER TOOL. To find this tool, simply type **'Google Keyword Planner Tool'** into the Google search bar.

To get access to the tool you'll need to create a google AdWords account. You don't have to pay for any advertising, but you do need to have an account. When you set up your account and login select the 'Tools and Analysis' menu option, followed by 'Keyword Planner'.

When you select Keyword planner you are given 3 options, as follows:

Keyword Planner
Plan your next search campaign

What would you like to do?

› Search for keyword and ad group ideas

› Enter or upload keywords to see how they perform

› Multiply keyword lists

As authors who are researching what people are searching for on the web we need to select **'Search for keyword and ad group ideas'.** Selecting this option will enable us to perform normal keyword research where we simply enter our **book idea keywords** and Google will then show us the searches people are making based on your keywords. The basic premise of this strategy is to determine whether or not people are searching for information based on our book subject. If they are, there is a good chance that your book will sell.

In the following image, which forms part of the Google Keyword Planner, you will be able to enter keywords and phrases based on your book subject idea(s). Once you have entered your keywords and phrases simply click 'GET IDEAS', and Google will tell you what people are searching for on Google, how many (approximately) searches there are, and also whether the competition is HIGH or LOW with regards to people advertising on Google through AdWords.

For example, when I was researching my 'how to become a pilot' book I found there to be 3,600 searches online every month with LOW competition. This immediately informed me that there was a potential gap in the market.

NOTE: Through research I have found that if people are searching for a specific area of information on Google, they will also be searching for it on Amazon, too.

You will see from the results on the following page that there are 3,600 average monthly searches for 'how to become a pilot' with LOW competition on AdWords. Although this LOW indicator does not mean there is LOW competition with regards to your book subject, it does mean there is LOW competition with regards to Google AdWords, which is something you may decide to use in order to promote your book online to reach a wider audience. I will give you more information about AdWords later on.

Results of Google searches based on the keyword phrase 'how to become a pilot'.

Your product or service		
how to become a pilot	Get ideas	Modify search

Ad group ideas	Keyword ideas		
Search Terms		Avg. monthly searches	Competition
how to become a pilot		3,600	Low

Please note: for those authors who are writing books in genres such as novels, fiction, mystery, crime and thriller etc, the Google Keyword Planner tool may not be much use to you as your book title will be very different to the ones that I personally create and search for. However, what is reassuring to know is that there are huge levels of search traffic on Amazon for your particular genre of book.

STEP 4 – GO TO AMAZON AND ASSESS THE COMPETITION

Step 4 in the research process is to go to Amazon and type the same book subject idea into the search bar near the top of the homepage. Prior to publishing the book 'how to become a pilot' I found there to be no competitors. If you go to Amazon.co.uk right now and type in 'how to become a pilot' you should see my book sitting at the number 1 spot in the search term. The reason why it is there at the number 1 spot is because it sells well, and it also matches the keyword phrase that you have typed into Amazon. Hopefully you can now see how effective my research strategy is, and also effective the Google Keyword Planner is.

What if there is lots of competition for the book subject I want to write about?

If you go to Amazon and find there to be many other books titled the same as your proposed book, do not be put off without considering the following first:

- If the competitor's book has poor reviews, this is an opportunity for you to create a better quality book.

- If the book cover design is sub-standard, this is an opportunity for you to create a better quality book.

I will be covering book cover design in detail in a later chapter, and you will read then about how important a book cover is to your overall book publishing strategy and success.

An example of how I beat the competition!

I think it would be useful for me to provide you with an example of a competitor's book I found on Amazon which I felt I could drastically improve on. I had carried out some research using the Google Keyword Planner tool and found there to be nearly 15,000 monthly searches for 'Armed Forces Tests'. Because I sell books based on careers within the Armed Forces, I decided that I wanted to create a testing book which provided the reader with sample Armed Forces Tests – unfortunately, when I followed step 4 of my strategy I found there to be a competitor's book selling tests on the same subject.

The competitor's book was very well established and had been selling strongly in the best-sellers list for some time. Despite this, I found a number of flaws with this particular book. To begin with, I felt the book cover was poor and that it did not do the content of the book justice. I also found another flaw with the book. The publisher had decided to call the book 'Practice tests for the Armed Forces'. When I returned to the Google Keyword Planner tool I found that there were ZERO monthly searches for this phrase. These two flaws gave me the confidence to create my own book on this subject. Here's what I did next:

1. I created a book which included more sample tests. In total, my book contained an additional 50 pages worth of tests than my competitors.

2. I improved the book cover to make it look both simple and professional.

3. I titled my book exactly what people were searching for – **ARMED FORCES TESTS** (approximately 15,000 monthly searches at the time).

4. I increased the price of my book by £5!

The reason why I increased the price of my book is because I am a genuine believer that in order to compete with another business you do not necessarily have to compete with them on the price. There are many people out there who will pay a premium for a book, product or service if they know they are going to get a better standard product or service.

My strategy worked, as I started to sell a lot more than my competitor's book – after a few months competing with me they decided to stop publishing their book.

MY ARMED FORCES TESTS BOOK COVER

If you have read this chapter, implemented my strategies, yet you still cannot come up with an idea for a book, I recommend you either attend one of my 1-day book writing and publishing courses or come and work with me on a one-to-one basis. Details for all of these options are listed below:

One-to-one coaching with Richard:

www.RichardMentorMe.com

Online Book Writing and Publishing Training Videos:

www.BookPublishingAcademy.co.uk

1-day book writing and publishing courses with Richard:

www.BookPublishingCourses.com

CHAPTER 4

HOW TO WRITE YOUR BOOK AND CREATE AN ACTION PLAN
(INCLUDING THE 11-HOUR PUBLISHING SYSTEM)

Get instant access to over 32 hours' worth of online training videos and support at:

www.BookPublishingAcademy.co.uk

HOW TO WRITE YOUR BOOK AND CREATE AN ACTION PLAN

In this chapter I will explain the process I go through when writing my books, including the action plan that I follow. Whilst I will also provide advice on chapters and the style of writing for various genres, your own style of writing is what will make your book unique. The way in which I write is not perfect, far from it, yet it is ideal for the genre of books I write. I have had no formal training or coaching with regards to my writing style as I want it to be as natural as possible and from the heart. So, the first piece of advice I want to give you in this chapter is to simply write in your own *style* and from the heart. It is this approach that will make your books unique. When it comes to the proofreading and editing stage, this is where any mistakes or errors will get identified and amended.

The action plan

Having an action plan will allow you to keep on track and get your book finished. You should decide before putting pen to paper, or fingers to key-board, how many pages you are going to write each day. My advice is to start off small and gradually build up as you feel your enthusiasm levels increasing and as your book starts to take shape. 300-400 words per day are sufficient in the beginning. John Grisham, one of the world's most successful authors, started his career as a lawyer. He used to get up very early every morning before work and write just one page.

Before you start writing your book you should have an outline of what the book will include. Personally, I write down all the proposed chapter titles on one page and then start to write the content for each one as and when I feel enthused. What's more, I do not necessarily always complete the chapters in chronological order. For example, when writing this book I completed the chapter on OUTSOURCING first, as this is a subject I feel very enthusiastic about, and I knew that once I had completed this chapter the rest would fall into shape.

The bottom line is there are no rules when it comes to writing a book – be creative and feel free to experiment. For my very first book (how to become a firefighter) I decided to include a chapter called **MY TOP 10 TIPS FOR SUCCESS.** This chapter has now featured in over 75% of my books, as my readers tell me it is one of the most useful sections.

When and where should you write?

I personally like to write at the end of the day, usually in the evening – I find I am at my most creative and productive during this time, and I am often still writing late into the night and through to the early hours. At the time of writing this chapter it is 2.35am! Only you will know what time is best for you to write. Like John Grisham, you may find you write more effectively very early in the morning before you go off to work. Take the time to think about the time of day you feel you would be best suited to writing, and then allocate this time into your schedule.

Some people like to write in bulk, and I can fully understand why they find this method stimulating. By writing in bulk I actually mean taking a few days or even a week out of their schedule and then blitzing the book in one go. This can sometimes be a useful strategy. From the money I have made through writing books I decided to buy a property in the Lake District, one of my all-time favourite locations. One of the reasons I bought this property is so that I have somewhere to go off to and write whenever I feel the urge to blitz a book. There are no distractions in the Lake District, and for me this is a great place to write.

If you have a family then I would recommend telling them that you are going to write a book. They will be able to encourage you and motivate you, and they will also hopefully give you some peace and quiet when you need it so that you can concentrate on your writing.

Get feedback along the way

During my training courses and one-to-one coaching sessions I will encourage all authors to seek feedback after they have completed each chapter. There is nothing worse than writing a book and then having to rewrite it because you didn't let anyone look at it. Have a mentor on hand to help you throughout the writing process. One other thing with regards to feedback – have thick skin! As an author you are putting your work out there to be read and reviewed. I can remember getting my first negative review on Amazon, and to be honest it really upset me. After a few days feeling sorry for myself I decided to turn the negative review into a positive situation. I engaged with the reviewer on Amazon and asked him to help me improve the book. He provided me with some tips on how he felt the book could be improved, and I took his comments on-board when writing the updated version.

Learn to hate procrastination

Procrastination is the action of delaying or postponing something – or in this case putting off writing your book. As authors we need to avoid this as much as possible. If you are the type of person who is likely to procrastinate then get yourself a mentor, or at least someone who will push and nag you to get your book completed.

I have never had a problem with procrastination, but I can understand why people do it. You just have to keep going and if you follow an action plan and stick it somewhere prominent, like on your fridge door, then you are far more likely to succeed. I usually find that once I have written three chapters of my book my motivation levels increase. At this stage I feel like I am making good progress, and once you get past the half way stage then the finishing line is in sight. Just keep focusing on seeing your book on sale in Waterstones and on Amazon and visualise the book flying off the shelves.

For those who want to write a novel

The first step when preparing to write a novel is to think about the types of book you really love; you know, the ones where you get lost in the story. Don't try to write a story about something that you think your friends or family will love; instead, write about what gets you going and what you are passionate about. You see, if you write about what you are passionate about then it will be easier to write from the heart and the book will sell better. We are aiming to make your writing a pleasurable and 'easy' experience. A great way to test what you are passionate about would be to write down a list of five things you are crazy about in your life. For me I just love helping people, which is why I enjoy writing career/self-help books that make a difference to others lives. Write down your list of five crazy obsessions and see if it doesn't inspire you to write.

The 'character'

When writing a novel you need to carefully consider the main character. You need to live with the character and learn to love them. If you do this your writing will be passionate. You should also consider making your character flawed in some manner. People love to read about exciting and unique characters as it takes them away from everyday life. You have to make your reader not want to put down the book. Of if they do put it down, they want to come back to it time and time again. You should also not be afraid to write in extremes. Take your character to places they shouldn't go to and allow them to do things they shouldn't be doing. Do not be afraid to experiment with scenarios and situations within your book, and try to be edgy. You can always take out parts or sections of the book later on if need be. Your character needs to be surprising you throughout your writing. If you do this you will maintain your reader's attention and enthusiasm. You should also try writing as if you are in character and in the present tense, the here and now.

Once you have decided on your character and his or her flaws, start your novel by writing a few lines with any of following beginnings, and then just see where it takes you:

"I have something to tell you and I don't think you are going to like it..."

"I have kept a secret for the last ten years and I can no longer keep hold of it..."

"On the surface he was every woman's dream; however...,"

"I have never told anyone this before..."

Of course, you can come up with your own beginnings for your novel, but I am sure you will find the above exercise helpful in getting started.

Your character has to have something going on in their life which is compelling. A great way to come up with this is to think about your friends and family. Do any of them have compelling problems either now or in the past that have caused major issues or problems? If so, you may decide to base your character on them without actually telling them. At the heart of every great story is usually a conflict or major issue – you should decide what that issue is before you start writing. The issue or problem should be close to your character throughout the book.

In order to maintain the readers interest levels your must keep the story going. By this I mean that you should write about something that is central to the 'plot' in just about every scene. The story needs to keep moving, and it is your job as an author to keep your readers interested by adding numerous twists and turns.

A great tip for writing novels is to ask yourself whether or not the storyline is believable. Even if you introduce ghosts and fairies you can still make the story believable by the style of writing you adopt. I can remember reading The Hobbit during my English Literature studies whilst at school, and the storyline was so believable I can still remember it to this day.

Don't follow any rules, and certainly don't follow my advice!

OK, so I'm probably sounding a little contradictory here. The point I am trying to make is that the novel is your book and nobody else's, therefore you can write it however you like.

Writing your manuscript

Most people will write their book/manuscript using Microsoft Word. If you are one of those people try writing in font style Arial or Times New Roman, font size 12 and with 1.5 paragraph spacing. The paragraph spacing is not essential, however a typesetter will usually use the same paragraph spacing when typesetting your book in preparation for print. If your manuscript is 200 pages in this format then the final finished 'typeset' version will not be too far from the same page length.

The structure of your book

Book structure is dependent on the genre of book you are writing. There are no hard and fast rules that you must follow, only guidelines. The general structure I use for my genre of book is as follows:

Title page – on this page I will include the main title of my book, the strapline, my company logo and the authors name.

Copyright and ordering information page – on this page I will always include my copyright notice and details of how people can order my books. It usually takes the following format:

Orders: Please contact How2become Ltd, Suite 3, 50 Churchill Square Business Centre, Kings Hill, Kent ME19 4YU. You can also order via the email address info@how2become.co.uk.

ISBN: 978-1-910202-05-0

First published in 2014 by How2Become Ltd.

Copyright © 2014 Richard McMunn. All rights reserved.

All rights reserved. Apart from any permitted use under UK copyright law no part of this publication may be reproduced or transmitted in any form or by any means, electronic or mechanical, including photocopying, recording, or any information, storage or retrieval system without permission in writing from the publisher or under licence from the Copyright Licensing Agency Limited. Further details of such licenses (for reprographic reproduction) may be obtained from the Copyright Licensing Agency Ltd, Saffron House, 6-10 Kirby Street, London EC1N 8TS.

NOTE: If you would like a copy of my book templates and copyright notices to use within your own book your can download them at my Book Publishing Academy: www.BookPublishingAcademy.co.uk

It is also good practice to include the name of the company which has printed your book on this page. Printing companies often have a tough time within the industry, and it is recognised as good practice if you promote them within your book on this page.

Foreword

Whilst a foreword is not a necessity, it can provide a useful 'lead in' to the main content of your book. The foreword will normally be written by someone of importance – perhaps a person in a position of authority.

The aim of the person writing the foreword is to introduce an author/work to the world, which can be accomplished in a variety of ways. The person writing the foreword could either write about a specific chapter in the book, the book as a whole (assuming they have read it), or the author's work in general. If they know the author personally then it is advisable that they talk about this relationship. If they don't, they could instead discuss how the author's work has affected their life or the importance of the work they are introducing.

If the person is writing a foreword to introduce a new edition of a book it is advisable that they talk about what's different in the current edition.

To help you, here is a sample foreword written by someone in a position of authority and expertise. This foreword was written for an author who I coached as part of my one-to-one coaching programme. His book, entitled **How to become a Driving instructor,** is available to view on Amazon.

Sample foreword

ABOUT BILL LAVENDER

Foreword by Robin Cummins OBE former DSA Chief Driving Examiner

This Guide has been written by industry insider, Bill Lavender. Well known for his "Better Training" features in adiNEWS for the last ten years, Bill became an Approved Driving Instructor in 1982 and has spent most of his career at the British School of Motoring (BSM) in various senior training and development roles, including NVQ and BTEC awards for instructors. He was also responsible for the company's learning resources, including retail products for learner drivers.

Bill now works freelance as an independent road safety consultant, specialising not only in driving instructor Continuing Professional Development (CPD), but also delivering Driver Certificate of Professional Competence (dCPC) courses for professional bus and lorry drivers. By producing this guide, Bill has reflected on his extensive knowledge and experience of the industry to provide first-hand guidance for anyone who is thinking about becoming an Approved Driving Instructor (ADI). Being a driving instructor is a very rewarding career for the right person. New learner drivers rely on good instructors who are suited to the job to not only prepare them to pass their tests first time, but also to help them enjoy the experience of learning how to stay safe on our busy roads.

The difference between the number of people first registering with the DSA to become an ADI and the number actually qualifying is a concern. There are clearly many people who must be very disappointed that they have not been able to qualify or have not been able to make a living out of the business for one reason or another.

It is important that every new potential instructor knows exactly what to expect from the industry, who is there to help you, and the best way to ensure that all expectations are fully met. As well as important technical information such as the lesson plans, you will find good advice on what it takes to be a successful instructor. There are many attractions to the job, and how well you do really does depend very much on how you use your personality and business acumen. To this extent, Bill has included details about ways to enhance your professional CV by entering into the world of qualified driver training.

This guide will help you decide whether to go ahead with the career or not, and whatever you decide it can help you save a lot of money and time. I would recommend this guide to every single potential driving instructor.

Robin Cummins OBE
Former DSA Chief Driving Examiner

Introduction or preface – A preface is your chance to speak directly to your readers about why you wrote the book, what the book is about, and why it's important. Fiction books do not require a preface. Here are a few useful tips on how to write one:

Within the preface discuss how the book came about. Tell the readers why you decided to write it, and also why you chose this particular subject. For example, when I wrote the preface to my 'how to become a firefighter' book I explained how people used to come and ask me for advice on joining the Fire Service, hence the reason I started writing the book. Within the preface you may also decide to include a brief description of the book. Do not give too much away, but instead give just enough to get the reader interested. Some authors also write about the problems they face when writing or researching the book and how they overcome those problems. The preface is also a great place to add your acknowledgements. Thank the people who supported you in writing your book, and don't forget to mention any proofreaders, mentors or editors.

Your preface should generally be quite short. The ones I write for my books are usually no more than five pages. You don't want the preface to drag on and on.

The main chapters of your book (consider up to 10 chapters) - the chapter titles will very much depend on the book genre and main title. For example, chapters for a book on interviews that I would write might be:

CHAPTER 1 – Why do employers use interviews?

CHAPTER 2 – The common mistakes made by people at interviews

CHAPTER 3 – The 10 main reasons why people fail at interviews

CHAPTER 4 – The interview scoring criteria

CHAPTER 5 – How you will be assessed at interviews

CHAPTER 6 – Sample interview questions and answers

CHAPTER 7 – How to easily beat the competition

CHAPTER 8 – 7 ways to impress the interview panel

CHAPTER 9 – Impressing with interview technique

CHAPTER 10 – Useful links and resources

You will notice that the first five chapters are generally negative – I use words such as 'mistakes' and 'fail' – this is deliberate. During the first half of the book I want to 'build the pain'. When it comes to the second half of the book I want to provide the solution. I use positive words and phrases such as 'easily beat the competition' and 'impress', which leaves the reader feeling upbeat and empowered to achieve.

Useful links and resources

I have found that most of my readers like me to include a 'useful links and resources' section towards the end of the book. This section will normally include website links and organisations which the reader will find useful. For example, at the end of this book I have provided a useful links and resources section that includes details of where to find book cover designers and typesetters etc. This will no doubt be useful information to you.

Disclaimers

I often get asked whether or not an author should include a disclaimer within their book. The answer will very much depend on the type of book he or she has written. For example, within many of my career-related books I will provide a simple disclaimer which states that I am not responsible for anyone failing any part of a selection process as a result of the content within my book. Whilst not essential, this does give me piece of mind, and it also informs the reader that they should only use my information as a guide.

In order to help you I have provided five sample disclaimers which you may be able to use within your particular book:

Sample book disclaimers

Some names and identifying details have been changed to protect the privacy of individuals.

(memoir or recent history)

This is a work of fiction. Names, characters, businesses, places, events and incidents are either the products of the author's imagination or used in a fictitious manner. Any resemblance to actual persons, living or dead, or actual events is purely coincidental.

(novels, short stories)

I have tried to recreate events, locales and conversations from my memories of them. In order to maintain their anonymity in some instances I have changed the names of individuals and places, I may have changed some identifying characteristics and details such as physical properties, occupations, and places of residence.

(memoir, autobiography)

Although the author and publisher have made every effort to ensure that the information in this book was correct at press time, the author and publisher do not assume and hereby disclaim any liability to any party for any loss, damage, or disruption caused by errors or omissions, whether such errors or omissions result from negligence, accident, or any other cause.

(advice, how-to)

This book is not intended as a substitute for the medical advice of physicians. The reader should regularly consult a physician in matters relating to his/her health, and particularly with respect to any symptoms that may require diagnosis or medical attention.

(health, alternative healing)

The information in this book is meant to supplement, not replace, proper (name your sport) training. Like any sport involving speed, equipment, balance and environmental factors, (this sport) poses some inherent risk. The authors and publisher advise readers to take full responsibility for their safety and know their limits. Before practicing the skills described in this book, be sure that your equipment is well maintained and do not take risks beyond your level of experience, aptitude, training, and comfort level.

(sports, training)

Sample action plan

I want to provide you with the exact same ACTION PLAN I have been using for the last few years to consistently publish high-quality books. So, without further ado, here it is:

STEP 1 – Generate your book idea

Using the tips supplied in the previous chapter start to create different ideas for your book. You may find it useful to use my BOOK IDEAS GENERATION FORM. Once you have come up with your book idea, write it down before moving onto step 2.

STEP 2 – Research to see whether or not the book will sell

During step 2 of the action plan you should use the Google Keyword Planner Tool to ascertain whether or not the book will sell. Type in the anticipated title of your book into the relevant field on the Planner Tool page using the lessons learnt during the previous chapter.

If you believe the book will sell and that there is demand for it, move on to step 3. If there are no people looking for your book, consider going back to step 1.

STEP 3 – Write the book

During step 3 you need to start writing the content for the book. As a general guide start writing your manuscript in Microsoft Word, font Arial size 12, with a paragraph spacing of 1.5. Set yourself a target of at least 3 pages every day. If you stick to this you will have written almost 100 pages within a month. Whilst you are writing your book move on to step 4.

STEP 4 – Order the front cover book design artwork

Whilst still writing your book, order the artwork for the front cover. I recommend reading the chapter relating to 'OUTSOURCERS' later on in the book to learn how to find great book cover designers.

STEP 5 – Proofreading and editing

Once you have finished writing the manuscript and you are 100% happy with the content, send it off to be proofread/edited. Once again, I recommend you refer to the 'OUTSOURCING' chapter to learn how to source professionals in this area.

STEP 6 – Typesetting and formatting for Kindle

Once the proofread/edited manuscript is returned to you and you have checked it over to see that you are happy with any changes made, it is now time to get the manuscript typeset for print and formatted for Kindle.

Typesetting is basically preparing the book for print. I recommend that you outsource this element of the book publishing process as it is important to get it right. I usually send the book cover design to the typesetter along with the manuscript so that he or she has an idea of how to brand and style the typesetting to maintain brand consistency. With regards Kindle formatting, I recommend you refer to chapter 10.

Please note: if you are opting to publish through **Amazon CreateSpace** then you will not be required to get your book typeset yourself – Amazon will do this for you (please refer to chapter 8).

STEP 7 – Open your Amazon account to get your book on pre-order

During step 7 of the action plan you will need to apply for your Amazon account. During chapter 8 I will explain the different options available to you. Before you open your Amazon account you will need to obtain your ISBN number from Nielsen, as you will need to allocate an ISBN to your book before Amazon will accept it (Advantage account holders only). If you are planning on opening a CreateSpace account then you will not need an ISBN, as Amazon will supply it for you. Your book can now go on pre-order sale by following the simple steps in your account.

STEP 8 – Open your Amazon Kindle Digital Text Platform (DTP) account and upload your book

During step 8 you need to get your formatted guide uploaded to Kindle. See chapter 10 for more details on how to do this following the simple steps in your account.

STEP 9 – Order your book cover jacket for print

During step 9 you are advised to order the full book cover jacket, which will be required for print. Although you already have the front cover, you will need the jacket, including spine and rear cover, for print purposes. Don't forget to also add the bar code and ISBN to the bottom right hand corner of the rear cover.

STEP 10 – Order your physical books from your chosen printer

Once you receive the typeset guide back from the designer you must check it over thoroughly to make sure there are no mistakes. Do not automatically assume the typesetter will not make any mistakes – they can and do creep in at times. Once you are happy with the typeset document and you have the full book cover jacket, you can now go to print. Whenever I order a new physical book from my printers I will always order a small run of approximately 100-200.

STEP 11 – Launch your physical book on Amazon and send a sample to Gardners books

As soon as you receive the printed books from the printers you can now launch your book on Amazon. You should also consider sending off a sample book to Gardners at this stage to see if they would be willing to stock it. There will be more about Gardners books later.

The above action plan has always worked for me, and I am sure it will work for you too. It does not matter what genre of book you are writing, give the action plan a try and see how far you get with your book writing and publishing aspirations.

THE 11-HOUR PUBLISHING METHOD FOR KINDLE

The 11-hour publishing method is an entirely different format of writing and publishing, which I designed to help those people who either have very little time to write or who find the physical act of writing difficult. Whilst the method is not for everyone, it is a useful strategy to have within your writing and publishing knowledge base and will help you get published on Kindle fast.

Writing vs. speaking

I can type at approximately 30 words per minute, whereas I can talk 5x faster at approximately 150 words per minute. Assuming I want to write a 50,000 word book, that will take me 1,666 minutes, or in excess of 27 hours. It is very difficult to do that all in one go! You will suffer 'writer's fatigue' and possibly become de-motivated in the process. Now, let's assume I want to speak 50,000 words. This will take me 332 minutes, or just in excess of 5.5 hours. It is far easier to do that all in one go. You will not suffer with fatigue and you will not become de-motivated.

The basis of the 11-hour publishing method is that you record the spoken content of your book as opposed to physically writing it. Once you have the recording of your spoken content you then take steps to get it transcribed, before finally proofreading, editing and publishing the entire book. Whilst this method will not suit all authors and self-publishers, I have found it to be a useful method for getting a book completed and published within a very short period of time. By following this method you will be able to complete and publish a book on Kindle in just 11 hours of your time.

In order to explain the 11-hour publishing method in greater detail, I have broken it down into the following steps.

STEP 1 (TIME = 2 HOURS) – The planning stage

Plan the content of your book by creating bullet point sections or chapters and then write them down on a sheet of paper.

STEP 2 (TIME = 5 HOURS) – The recording stage

Start to record just one section or chapter of your book at a time by using a suitable voice recorder, such as your iPhone/smartphone (see below). Don't worry about making mistakes as these will be edited and rectified before you publish the book.

Using your iPhone to record voice

1 – Go to Utilities / Voice memos

2 – Start recording (record just one chapter at a time for a max of 20 minutes)

3 – Immediately after recording the audio, save the file to your phone.

4 – Now send the audio file directly to yourself via email using the phone.

5 – Save the audio file on your desktop using a name that is relevant to the content, e.g. Chapter 1, Chapter 2 etc.

STEP 3 (TIME = 30 MINS) – The transcription stage

Sign up for an account at www.Speechpad.com and upload your files for transcription. Transcription involves listening to a recording of something and typing the contents up into a document, which is then returned to the client, giving them a written record of what's on the recording. On speechpad.com, it cost me just £54.46 to get 18,000 words transcribed.

STEP 4 (TIME = 30 MINS) – Order your book artwork

Whilst waiting for the transcription to be completed and returned to you, you can order the front cover artwork for your book.

STEP 5 (TIME = 2 HOURS) – Proofreading and editing

Once your transcription is returned from speechpad.com you need to spend time editing the content, not just to check for errors but also to amend the content so that it 'reads' exactly how you want it to. As you will be aware, we speak differently to how we write, and you will need to edit the content for this reason. Alternatively, send it off to a professional proofreader/editor who will complete this stage for you.

STEP 6 (TIME = 15 MINS) – Conversion for Kindle

Once your edited content is complete you need to get someone qualified to format the book in ePub for Kindle.

STEP 7 (TIME = 45 MINS) – Upload your book to Kindle

Once you have the formatted file back from the outsourcer you can upload the book to Kindle for publication.

TOTAL TIME = 11 hours

This method can be used in conjunction with traditional writing too. For example, you could try writing a few chapters in the traditional method and the remainder using the 11-hour method. I have also found that the 11-hour method is perfect for writing blog articles for my website, which are then used to help promote my book(s). Give it a try and see how you get on.

Now let's take a look at the important subject of creating book cover designs and book titles.

CHAPTER 5
DESIGNS AND BOOK TITLES

Get instant access to over 32 hours' worth of online training videos and support at:

www.BookPublishingAcademy.co.uk

BOOK COVER DESIGNS AND BOOK TITLES

In this particular chapter I am going to cover the important subject of book cover designs and titles. As you will have gathered so far during the content of the book, these two subjects are profoundly important with regards to the success of your writing and publishing strategy.

Whilst I have covered the subject of book titles during chapter 3 – 'Researching ideas for book subjects', I want to cover it again here, but this time in more detail with a case study. Therefore some elements of this chapter will be repeated.

Book titles

Your chosen book title can have a huge impact on the number of books that you sell. You will note that my philosophy for choosing books titles is very much focused on what people are searching for online. The internet is here to stay, and as such you need to focus your strategy on putting your book right under the noses of your customers. If you give people what they are looking for you will sell lots of books. First of all, let's revisit my own strategy for choosing book titles.

Step 1 – Create your book idea

The first step is to use the strategies and tips provided in chapter 3 to generate your book idea.

As mentioned previously, a great way to find hot book ideas is to spend time reading the newspapers. Let's assume you have been reading the newspapers one Sunday afternoon, and you notice the following headline:

The headline and story clearly indicates that more and more people are starting up home-based business. The headline and text to the left actually featured in THE TIMES during early 2014, and I saw this as an opportunity for someone to write a book.

Step 2 – Use the Google Keyword Planner to determine search traffic for this subject

Using the methods described in chapter 3, I will now go direct to the Google **Planner Keyword Tool** facility in order to determine what people are searching for online.

I soon realise that there are people searching for information around this subject:

There are approximately 30,340 searches in the **Ad Group** category for "How to start a business from home", and when you drill down further using the **Keyword Ideas** button you will notice that there are 210 average monthly searches for this particular phrase. Whilst this is not a huge number of people searching for this subject, it is still healthy.

The great thing about the keyword planner tool is that I am also able to see what the searches are like on a month-by-month basis; or in other words, I can determine whether or not there are any seasonal hikes in search traffic. In order to achieve this simply hover your mouse over the small icon to the left of the average monthly searches figure – the icon looks very similar to a small graph.

If I hover over the search phrase "How to start a business from home", a graph will appear which looks like the following:

Monthly searches for the last 12 months
Stats also available with downloads

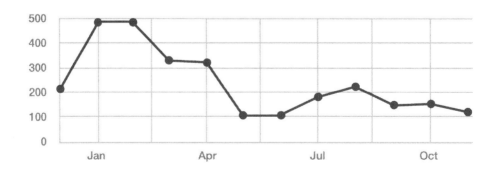

From this graph I can determine that the searches for this particular search phrase literally double in January and February. This tells me that I will probably sell more of this type of book at the start of the New Year, as people are probably looking for a fresh start. This type of information will also help me to plan ahead with regards to how much physical stock I have available in order to meet demand.

Step 3 – Go to Amazon.co.uk and see if there is any competition

Once I have determined there is healthy search traffic for my chosen book subject I will now go to Amazon to see whether there is any competition, and if it is worth competing in this particular niche.

At the time of writing there are many books available on starting up business, but not one entitled "How to start a business from home". This tells me that there is a gap in the market for a book with this subject.

Creating a strapline

Whenever I consider a title for my book I will almost always add a strapline. A strapline is an extra few words which describe what the book is. Here are a few main book titles, followed by straplines highlighted in grey:

How to become a Firefighter: The ULTIMATE guide to PASSING the Firefighter Selection process

Teacher Interview Questions: Advice and Strategies for PASSING the Teacher Interview

Psychometric Test Questions: 500 Sample Test Questions and Answers

How to Start a Business from Home: Step-by-step advice on starting a home-based BUSINESS

You will notice that I have made use of 'power words' in the first two book title examples – 'ultimate' and 'passing'. You will also notice that I have capitalised these words. I have found that capitalising one or two power words in the strapline helps with conversions. It is certainly worth being creative with your strapline, as this will help your book to standout from any competitors within your niche.

Another useful way to increase the sales of your book or sell more than your competitors is to actually put the current year/version of the book in the strapline. For example, at the time of writing the current year is 2014. For my firefighter book I will call it:

How to become a Firefighter: The ULTIMATE guide to PASSING the Firefighter Selection process, 2014 version

You will notice that by simply adding '2014 version' to the end of my strapline it automatically makes the book feel fresh and up-to-date. Now, of course, you can only actually add this to your strapline if the book is a 2014 version. With most of my books I will update them every year, which qualifies me to add this extra element to my book(s).

Using numbers in book titles

The use of numbers in book titles, especially for books within genres such as self-help, fitness, motivation, property and business start-up, can be extremely useful in helping with conversions.

Everyone in society is busy. We only a have a few spare moments each day to read books and dedicate time to our own self-development, therefore a book which offers to teach you something within a set time-period can be an advantage. Let me give you some examples of book titles, first of all without the number(s) and then with:

BOOK TITLE WITHOUT NUMBERS	BOOK TITLE WITH NUMBERS
How to do press ups	7 weeks to 100 press-ups
How to make money	4 ways to make £1,000 in a week
How to start a business	How to set up a Business in 7 Days from scratch
Yoga for beginners	12 weeks to Yoga success
Job interview questions and answers	147 job interview questions and answers
How to motivate yourself	97 different ways to motivate yourself

You can instantly see how the inclusion of numbers within a book title makes the book more valuable and sellable. The customer can automatically 'feel' the value of the book as they can see an end result. I also find that the use of the number 7 is rather useful when creating book titles, simply because the vast majority of people associate this number with luck. Including numbers within book titles will also help you to write and construct the book. If you have a specific number to work towards when writing your manuscript then the book will be far easier to write.

EXAMPLES OF GOOD BOOK COVERS

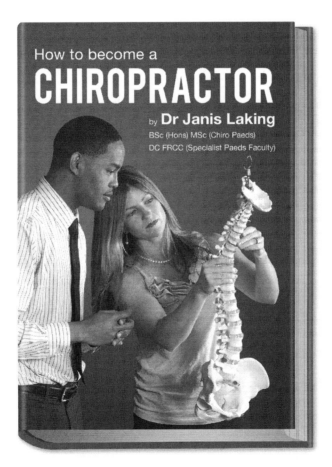

How to become a Chiropractor by Dr Janis Laking

Why is this cover good?

To begin with, the title is simple, effective, and matches what people are searching for on the internet. The cover also provides the authors qualification, which builds trust and confidence between the customer and the author. If trust and confidence are built a sale is more likely to take place. The image on the front cover clearly shows a teacher and student scenario, which is relevant to the book subject. Customers can easily identify what the book subject is without opening it up to read it.

Who designed this cover?

www.BookPublishingAcademy.co.uk

How to become a Game Designer by Joshua Brown

Why is this cover good?

The dark/professional colours of blue and black work well with the white text on this book cover. The text 'GAME DESIGNER' stands out prominently on the cover, sending a clear message to the customer what the subject is about. The image of the girl shows she is 'ready to start working' on her journey to becoming a Game Designer. The designer of the cover also added a logo to this book as it forms part of a series. Space invader images were also used on the cover, as most people will relate to these when thinking of video games.

Who designed this cover?

www.BookPublishingAcademy.co.uk

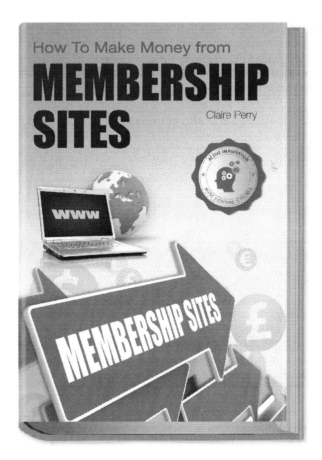

How to make money from membership sites by Claire Perry

Why is this cover good?

The cover utilises bold/large text and gives a clear message which shows what the book subject is about. Again, the book subject is simple and representative of what people are searching for online. The large arrows towards the bottom half of the book cover draw the reader to open the book and explore the subject matter within. The designer has also made good use of 'WWW' and the computer screen to further illustrate the book subject matter.

Who designed this cover?

www.BookPublishingAcademy.co.uk

A step-by-step guide for beating Anorexia and Bulimia by Beverley Marais

Why is this cover good?

The cover is designed in sky blue with 'soft' clouds. This has been done deliberately in order to create a soft and approachable feel. The author of the book, Beverley Marais, also features on the front cover of the book to build trust and rapport between herself and the reader. This approach will also make any up-sells easier as the reader can see the author and relate to her.

Who designed this cover?

www.BookPublishingAcademy.co.uk

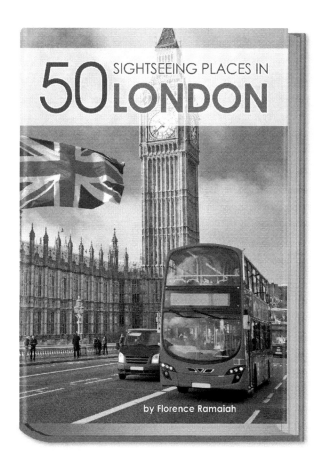

50 sightseeing places in London

Why is this cover good?

The book's target audience will most probably be visitors to the UK from abroad. Therefore, the images used on the cover needed to be highly relevant to what people would immediately think of when they think of the City of London. When creating this book cover the designer surveyed 30 people and asked them all to write down three objects or places they immediately thought of when thinking of London. During the survey, the majority of people listed the Union Jack flag, a double-decker bus and Big Ben.

Who designed this cover?

www.BookPublishingAcademy.co.uk

GETTING THE FULL BOOK COVER JACKET CREATED

At some point during the book publishing process you will need to get the full book cover jacket created in preparation for print. If you only intend publishing your book through the Kindle platform then you will not need to do this.

In order to order the full book cover jacket you will need the following:

1. The spine width.

2. The text that you want to be included on your spine, including any logo.

3. The rear text for your book, including any images.

4. International Standard Book Number.

5. The bar code.

I will now go through each of the above five elements and explain what they are.

The spine width

The way you can ascertain the width of your book spine is to count the number of pages of your typeset book. To give you a rough idea for books that will be digitally printed, I have provided a sample chart on the following page which includes the number of pages (page extent) and the spine width in millimetres based on a paper quality of 80GSM.

PAGE EXTENT	80GSM AMBER PREPRINT
64	4.5
72	5
80	5.5
88	6
96	6.5
104	6.5
112	7
120	7.5
128	7.5
136	8
144	8.5
152	9
160	9.5
168	9.5
176	10
184	10.5
192	11
200	11.5
208	11.5
216	12
224	12.5
232	13
240	13.5
248	13.5
256	14
264	14.5
272	15
280	15.5
288	16
296	16.5
304	16.5
312	17
320	17.5
328	18
336	18.5
344	18.5
352	19
360	19.5
368	20
376	20.5

To give you an example using the chart, if your book is 112 pages long you will need to get your full book cover jacket designed with a 1mm spine. Please note: if your page extent falls between two numbers, always round up to the next spine width thickness.

The text that you want to be included on your spine, including any logo

The text that you want to be included on the spine should normally be the TITLE of your book, the authors name, and also a small logo.

The rear text for your book, including any images

There are no rules as to what text you should include on the rear cover; however, to help you decide, the following is an example of what I would normally write:

SAMPLE REAR TEXT FOR YOUR BOOK COVER

How to become a driving instructor is the definitive resource for anyone wishing to obtain a highly sought after career within the driving industry.

The benefits of being a driving instructor are many and varied. You can choose your own working hours and have control over how long your working week is. You will need certain qualities in order to become a driving instructor, such as patience, flexibility, honesty, punctuality, restraint, and diplomacy, amongst others. This guide will teach you how to become a driving instructor, from how to start out, the different training options, lesson plans, and also the different routes available to you in respect of working alone or working through an established driving school.

The guide has been created by driving school professionals to bring you the very best in expert information and advice.

MAIN PRODUCT FEATURES

- 330 pages of expert information and tutorials

- How and where to train as a driving instructor

- The ULTIMATE guide for aspiring driving instructors

- Written by a leading expert within the driving instructor industry

About the Author

Bill Lavender is well known for his BETTER TRAINING features in the industry magazine, adiNEWS over the last ten years. He became an Approved Driving Instructor in 1982 and has spent most of his career at the British School of Motoring (BSM) in various senior training and development roles, including NVQ and BTEC awards for instructors. He also was responsible for BSM learning resources, including retail products for learner drivers.

Some authors will also list the different chapters on the rear text and include a photograph. Like I say, there are no rules, and it is entirely up to you what you add to the rear cover of your book.

TIP: if you have a website or blog then the rear text is a great place to promote these. Always consider adding your website or blog URL to the rear cover of your book. You should also include a 'call to action' which will serve to encourage the reader to visit your website. An example of this might be:

"Visit Richard McMunn's website to get access to 32 hours' worth of online training videos and support: www.BookPublishingAcademy.co.uk"

International Standard Book Number

The International Standard Book Number (ISBN) is a 13-digit number that uniquely identifies books and book-like products published internationally. The purpose of the ISBN is to establish and identify one title or edition of a title from one specific publisher, and it is unique to that edition, thus allowing for more efficient marketing of products by booksellers, libraries, universities, wholesalers and distributors.

Every ISBN consists of thirteen digits, and whenever it is printed it is preceded by the letters ISBN. The thirteen-digit number is divided into four parts of variable length, each part separated by a hyphen. The ISBN will usually go just above the bar code in the bottom right hand corner of the rear cover.

There is a piece of software which will create your barcode for you for free. You can download the software from:

http://www.nchsoftware.com/barcode/

The barcode, once generated with your own unique ISBN, will look something like this:

It is important that the ISBN is also included above the bar code.

SAMPLE FULL BOOK COVER JACKET

To give you an idea of how the full jacket cover should look, here is one that I created for one of my clients:

GETTING YOUR BOOKS PRINTED

Within the publishing industry you basically have a couple of printing options, which are listed as follows:

1. Digital (print-on-demand, POD)

2. Litho.

Both have their advantages and disadvantages in terms of cost and quality. Whenever I publish a book I will usually opt for digital printing, as it enables me to order fewer copies. This enables me to reduce the risk in terms of the initial outlay whilst I test the market to see how many units the book will sell. If the book is a big seller I will then order litho copies as these are slightly cheaper, but you do need to order larger runs.

Printing technology has come a long way in the last 15 years. It's been something of a revolution in the industry, with digital printing starting to replace the more traditional ink based litho printing in many areas. The reason for this is simply because, as a self-publisher, you can produce good quality results in small quantities at a reasonable cost. Previously the set up costs alone on a litho printing press would have meant that at least 500 copies of a book would have to be printed (most printers wouldn't print fewer at that time and still do not), making the entry costs quite high.

Which option is best for a self-published book?

The answer is that it depends on what you are hoping to achieve and how much you want to risk. There are two basic options:

1. Digital printing (POD), which is great for small numbers of books or if you are only expecting to sell a relatively small number of copies. Digital printing is effectively a very large laser printer combined with a binding line.

2. Litho printing (ink-based printing), which is better for a larger number of books. This is the traditional form of printing that has been used to produce books for centuries.

My advice is to opt for digital printing initially until you know how many books you are going to need in the long run. If you join my Book Publishing Academy at the following website then you will have access to my printer and be able to get the same competitive rates that I get for digital printing:

www.BookPublishingAcademy.co.uk

Now let's move onto the next chapter, which is entitled 'Books for Business Owners'.

CHAPTER 6
BOOKS FOR BUSINESS OWNERS

Get instant access to over 32 hours' worth of online training videos and support at:

www.BookPublishingAcademy.co.uk

BOOKS FOR BUSINESS OWNERS

One of the problems new business start-ups will experience when starting their new business is a level of frustration. This means frustration at not being able to move forward as quickly as they might want. Any new business needs solid foundations if it is to become sustainable.

It is pointless building a new business that is successful in its first year and then fails in the following year due to a lack of initial planning and fore-sight. When a builder builds a house he makes sure the foundations are laid and fully dry before he begins to lay his bricks on top. Use this analogy when building your business. Create solid foundations in terms of financial management, product quality, and customer service standards before you move forward. These are the type of things that can come back to haunt you if you fail to put effective systems in place very early on.

In order to give you an idea of the number of businesses that fail in the early years, take a look at the following chart.

Percentage of business that fail in the first years of trading

YEAR	PERCENT FAILED
YEAR 1	25%
YEAR 2	36%
YEAR 3	44%
YEAR 4	50%
YEAR 5	55%
YEAR 6	60%
YEAR 7	63%
YEAR 8	66%
YEAR 9	69%
YEAR 10	71%

You will notice that after just four years of trading half of all business start-ups have failed. There a number of reasons why this happens. In no particular order:

Reason for failure #1 – A lack of credibility and authority

When I was working in the Royal Navy or the Fire Service I was just a number. Nobody knew of me apart from my work colleagues, friends and family. Whilst this approach was fine as an 'employee', it does not work as an 'entrepreneur'.

One of the main reasons why I have become successful so quickly in business is because I have made myself 'visible'. I have also deliberately made myself the 'authority' within my chosen niche, and I have achieved this through writing books.

"Whatever business you are in, I strongly recommend you write a book."

Let me give you an example in the following case study:

HOW WRITING A BOOK CAN HELP YOU IN ANY BUSINESS – A CASE STUDY

Steven runs a second hand car sales business which operates from a garage forecourt and online via his website. He is doing quite well and generating sales of £850,000 per year. However, there are a number of competitors in the local area and he wants to increase his revenues by taking business from his competitors.

He approaches me for business mentoring, and I recommend that he writes a book in order to help him gain credibility and authority – something which his competitors do not have. After spending time with him during the initial one-to-one consultation I determine that one of his strengths is his customer service. I advise him to write a book entitled:

"How to Get the Best Deal When Buying a Second Hand Car"

Steven looks at me in a bemused manner and says...

"But if I write a book on this subject I will be telling my customers how they can get money off when buying a car."

My response is ...

"Exactly... if you follow this approach then you will sell more cars and take more business from your competitors because you will be building a relationship with your customers, and also one more very important thing – trust. Once you have written this book I would then encourage you to give a free copy of the book to every person who walks through your showroom doors. When you give them the book, tell them that you wrote the book to help them get the best deal possible when buying a car."

As soon as I said this I could see the penny drop by the reaction on Steven's face. I carried on:

"You see, Steven; trust is a very important thing in any business. It's one thing getting a customer to come to your car showroom or your website, but getting them to part with potentially thousands of pounds is another. If the customer feels they can trust you they will do business with you, time and time again. Not only that, but by writing your book you will be giving yourself more credibility as an entrepreneur and business owner."

I have helped many business owners to gain credibility and authoritativeness through writing books. Remember, if you own a business or intend starting one, writing and publishing a book is a sure-fire way to get you and your business known quickly. It will also add credibility and authority to your business, and it can ensure sustainability for many years to come.

Let's now move onto one of my favourite subjects in publishing, Amazon.

CHAPTER 7
ABOUT AMAZON

Get instant access to over 32 hours' worth of online training videos and support at:

www.BookPublishingAcademy.co.uk

ABOUT AMAZON

Amazon has taken the world by storm ever since it was founded by Jeff Bezos back in 1995. It essentially dominates and drives the publishing industry and has been responsible for bringing us the highly successful Kindle. There are many people and organisations within the publishing industry who detest Amazon, simply because they take such a high percentage from authors and publishers alike. My view on Amazon is different, however – I think they are brilliant and an essential marketplace in which to sell your books to a massive audience. Where else can your book go on sale to a potential 80,000,000 customers every month? If you understand Amazon and how it works you can actually make it work to your advantage, which I will explain in detail during this and the next chapter.

Background to Amazon

In order to understand Amazon and how it can help us to sell thousands of books, we need to first of all understand its history. Amazon was founded in 1995 by Jeff Bezos, and it was initially an online book retailer. Books were the very first product which Amazon sold, and it is 'books' which drive the business forward today, despite the fact that they now sell virtually anything and everything!

Amazon was initially called **Abracadabra** because Jeff wanted to sell every product from the alphabet, but the name was soon changed to **Amazon** because the Amazon is the longest river in the world, it starts with the letter 'A' (something which Jeff wanted), and it represents significant 'volume' and 'depth'.

Over recent years a large number of High Street booksellers have either gone into administration, or if they haven't, they have seen their profits drop significantly. The main reason for this is twofold:

1. Consumers are choosing to buy their books and general goods online – this trend will continue;

2. Amazon offers consumers excellent customer service and fast delivery at low prices.

High Street bookstores simply cannot compete with Amazon for the following reasons:

1. A standard bricks and mortar High Street book store can hold approximately 200,000 physical books, whereas Amazon can stock unlimited numbers of books;

2. With more and more consumers switching to the internet in order to buy their books and other goods, High Street book stores will suffer and will continue to do so;

3. Because Amazon is not a 'face-to-face' retailer it is able to keep its costs down and offer exceptional customer service;

4. Due to the unbelievably large number of transactions Amazon takes everyday it is able to negotiate excellent postal rates with the likes of Royal Mail and other mail/package delivery companies. This effectively enables Amazon to offer FREE postage and package to its customers;

5. High Street bookstores are not very good at 'capturing' customer's details when they walk through their shop front door. This is a shame, because it is these details which could be used for future marketing promotions. Once you buy one product from Amazon they will then email you every week to offer you extra goods and products – this is called the 'upsell'.

Amazon customer service

The Amazon logo represents a large 'smile', which indicates how obsessed they are with providing great customer service. If you complain to Amazon as a customer, they will either sort it out for you ASAP or refund your payment. Their exceptional level of customer service is another reason why Amazon has done so well. Ask yourself the following question – how many times have you received poor customer service from a High Street shop? I have experienced it many times in the past, yet I have never received poor customer service from Amazon.

Now ask yourself another question – how many times have you gone to buy products from a High Street store to find that they don't have your size or what you want in stock? Again, this has happened to me many times, and all it does is force me to shop online with retailers such as Amazon where I know they will have what I want and will be able to deliver within 24 hours.

The great thing about selling your books on Amazon is that this outstanding level of customer service is all set up to help you. You do not have to employ any staff. You do not have to send your books to your customers, and you also do not have to deal with any customer service enquiries or complaints – Amazon will do all of this for you.

Interestingly enough, Amazon took six years to turn a profit. This is because it is always looking at ways to dominate the market and create innovative products, such as the Kindle. Do you remember when the Kindle first came to market in 2007? Our television screens were inundated with TV adverts by Amazon promoting their new product – since then they have changed the way we 'read'. Whilst the sale of printed books is still on the rise on Amazon, Kindle sales are outstripping them by more than 2:1.

Amazon acquisitions

Amazon has been busy buying many different businesses over the years in an attempt to maintain its dominance in the online market. Below are just a few examples of companies and business which have been purchased by Amazon:

1998: Bookpages.co.uk, a UK online book retailer, which became Amazon UK on October 15.

1999: Internet Movie Database (IMDb). PlanetAll, a reminder service based in Cambridge, Massachusetts; Junglee.com, an XML-based data mining start-up based in Sunnyvale; Alexa Internet, Accept.com, and Exchange. com.

2003: Online music retailer CD Now.

2004: Joyo.com, a Chinese e-commerce website.

2005: BookSurge, a print on demand company, and Mobipocket.com, an eBook software company.

CreateSpace.com (formerly CustomFlix), a distributor of on-demand DVDs, based in Scotts Valley, California. CreateSpace has since expanded to include on-demand books, CDs, and video.

2006: Shopbop, a retailer of designer clothing and accessories for women, based in Madison, Wisconsin.

2007: dpreview.com, a digital photography review website based in London; Brilliance Audio, the largest independent publisher of audiobooks in the United States.

2008: Audible.com; Fabric.com; Box Office Mojo; AbeBooks; Shelfari; (including a 40% stake in LibraryThing and whole ownership of BookFinder.

com, Gojaba.com, and FillZ); Reflexive Entertainment, a casual video game development company.

2009: Zappos, an online shoe and apparel retailer, Lexcycle.

2010: Touchco., Woot, Quidsi, BuyVIP, Amie Street.

2011: Lovefilm, The Book Depository, Pushbutton.

If you want to reach maximum exposure for you book(s) then you must sell them on Amazon.

The Amazon loss leader

For those people who understand sales and marketing, you will undoubtedly be familiar with the term 'loss leader'. A loss leader can be described as:

"A product sold at a low price (at cost or below cost) to stimulate other profitable sales."

Amazon is the master of the loss leader. It uses 'books' as a way to draw customers into their database and, once a person has made their first purchase, they will then try to sell them additional goods both immediately on their sales-page and also by way of email promotions after the initial purchase.

If you have previously purchased something from Amazon, start to take note of how often they email you with follow-up offers and promotions – they are extremely clever at what they do, and as an author/self-publisher you are going to take advantage of their outstanding marketing systems.

CHAPTER 8

HOW TO SELL YOUR BOOKS ON AMAZON

Get instant access to over 32 hours' worth of online training videos and support at:

www.BookPublishingAcademy.co.uk

HOW TO SELL YOUR BOOKS ON AMAZON

During this next chapter I am going to teach you how to sell your book(s) on Amazon. Now that we know a little about Amazon's history and how it works we can start to put the pieces of the selling process together. To begin with, let's take a look at the Amazon sales-page.

The Amazon sales-page explained

When you next go to the Amazon website, take a look at any page on their site that is selling a book. On each sales page there are a number of **POINTS OF INTEREST,** which I believe you need to fully understand when self-publishing books:

POINT OF INTEREST 1: The book title

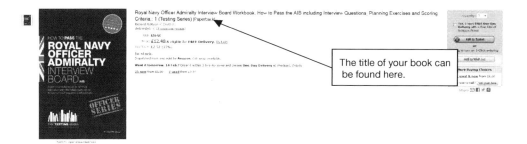

The title of your book has a significant impact on how your book will be listed on Amazon, and also in the natural search engines such as Google and Bing. As we established earlier, we need to name our book with a phrase that is relevant to what people are searching for, both on the search engines and also on Amazon. For example, if I wanted to write and publish a book that teaches people **how to write a business plan** for a new business, I would call it one of the following:

- How To Write A Business Plan
- How To Write A Business Plan: An ESSENTIAL guide for NEW Business Start-Ups
- How To Write A Business Plan: The ULTIMATE guide for writing Business Plans
- How To Write A Business Plan for Beginners

You will notice that I have used the main focus of the book (how to write a business plan) at the start of the overall title. This is for the following reasons:

1. This title is easy to understand, and it tells the customer EXACTLY what the book is about and what it will do for them;

2. I want the search engines and Amazon to list this book on the first page for the phrase 'how to write a business plan'. If the book title is 'relevant' to what people are searching for it will have a better chance of ranking in the search pages on Google and Amazon.

To give you an example of how I have used this method to great success over the years, here is a sample case study:

In 2013 I worked closely with an author called Bill Lavender through my one-to-one coaching programme to help him publish his book that teaches people how to become a driving instructor. Bill is a highly experienced driving instructor, and he wanted to publish a book that would help people achieve their goal. I initially carried out some research using the Google Keyword Planner tool and established that 6,600 people were searching for the phrase 'how to become a driving instructor'.

I then turned my attentions to Amazon and found that no other author or publisher was selling a book using the same title. There were, however, a small number of people selling books on the same subject, albeit with different titles such as:

- The Driving Instructors Handbook

- Become an Approved Driving Instructor

- How to land a top-paying Driving Instructors job

Now, I am not saying that these titles are poor, because they are not. I am also not saying that the books will not sell, far from it. What I am saying is that my strategy and approach for naming books exactly what people are searching for makes perfect sense, and it works. If you create a product or service and then put it right under the noses of the customers who are searching for it you will have a better chance of making a sale. If you go to Amazon.co.uk right now and type in 'how to become a driving instructor' you will see Bill's book right at the top of the listings for that search term.

It is important that I point out at this stage that just because you name a book exactly what your customers are searching for, it will not automatically equal a rank at number 1 spot for that search term. There are other important factors that have an influence, too, such as the reviews, the number of sales, and also the number of books your book is **frequently bought together** with.

POINT OF INTEREST 2: The front cover design of the book

When selling on Amazon, and online in general, you should always aim for simplicity and quality. When a person visits a website or sales-page you literally have just a few seconds to gain their interest in your product or service. If you do not gain their interest they will go elsewhere. To prove this point, I encourage you to think carefully about how you personally search for goods and services online and how long you stay on a particular website whilst surfing. When you next search the web for a particular product or service, think about those websites that make you stay and ask yourself the question – 'what makes me stay on this website?' It might be the quality of the website you are visiting, the level of trust it offers, or more likely it will be the fact that they offer exactly what you are looking for.

With regards to your book cover, try to think about your customers and what they would want. Too many authors and publishers create book covers that have little relevance to the book title or subject. Your job, remember, is to make the customer click the BUY NOW button, and creating quality and relevant book covers will certainly help with the conversion rate.

POINT OF INTEREST 3: The book's description

Your books description will be shown here.

The book description is your opportunity to 'sell' your book to the customer. Most customers will read the description before deciding whether or not to click the BUY NOW button, therefore it is important that it is free from mistakes, grammatically correct, and uses positive words to describe how the book will be of benefit to the reader. Here are some great tips that will help you to construct a great book description:

TIP 1. When writing the book description, the only thing that matters is the main plot or main theme of the book. Do not overcomplicate the description, and always consider the fact that the customer will want to make a relatively fast decision on whether or not to buy your book.

TIP 2. Keep it under 200 words. There are no rules with regards to how long or short your description should be, but I have tested both very short descriptions and also ones that are in excess of 500 words. In summary, I have found that those that are between 150 and 200 words convert better. In the simplest terms, when writing your book description, concentrate on what your book is about and what your readers will find interesting about it. You may also find it useful to include the chapter titles within your description.

TIP 3. Write in third person, present tense. When describing your book think as if you are sitting face-to-face with the reader. Pretend they have asked you what the book is about and you are telling them.

TIP 4. Repeat the title of the book 2-3 times in the description, but no more. When writing my book descriptions I will always start off with the title of the book. I will then include it one or two times more throughout the duration of the description. The reason that I do this is solely for search engine optimisation purposes, as I want the books sales-page to rank on the major search engines for the title of the book.

TIP 5. Use emotional 'power words' in the description. My advice would be to use approximately 5-10 power words within your books description. Power words are used to evoke emotion, and they will certainly help to increase conversions. Just make sure the power words are relevant to the content of your book, and also relevant to your books genre.

Examples of power words for novels and fiction books include:

Amazing, Audacity, Backbone, Belief, Blissful, Bravery, Breathtaking, Cheer, Conquer, Courage, Daring, Defiance, Delight, Devoted, Excited, Eye-opening, Faith, Fearless, Fulfil, Grateful, Grit, Guts, Happy, Heart, Hero, Hope, Jaw-dropping, Jubilant, Magic, Mind-blowing, Miracle, Pluck, Sensational, Spectacular, Spirit, Stunning, Surprising, Triumph, Uplifting, Valour, Victory, Wonderful and Wondrous.

Examples of power words for self-help, motivational and business start-up books include:

Accomplished, Attentive, Benevolent, Bold, Bright, Brilliant, Captivating, Caring, Compassionate, Conscious, Constant, Courageous, Courteous, Dedicated, Determined, Disciplined, Effective, Energetic, Engaging, Entertaining, Enthusiastic, Equitable, Expressive, Exquisite, Extraordinary, Fascinating, Fearless, Flexible, Fortunate, Friendly, Generous, Genuine, Glorious, Gracious, Gutsy, Helpful, Honourable, Immense, Incredible, Ingenious, Inspiring, Intelligent, Intuitive, Inventive, Majestic, Marvellous, Motivating, Optimistic, Original, Passionate, Perceptive, Persistent, Pleasing, Powerful, Quick-minded, Remarkable, Resourceful, Rousing, Sensational, Sincere, Stunning, Understanding, Unique and Venturous.

TIP 6. Write the description as if you are the publisher, not the author. Making an impact on the reader is your principal concern. Your job is to make sure the reader finishes reading the description with a desire to want to find out more. Remember, the book description is marketing material - not literature.

POINT OF INTEREST 4: Book reviews and Amazon Verified Purchases

Amazon Verified Purchases can help your books rankings.

Book reviews have a massive impact on the number of units you will sell. I have known a number of authors to spend months, sometimes years, writing their book; only for it to receive 1 or 2 star reviews once it is published, and the book sales plummet as a consequence.

There is no golden formula for getting positive reviews for your book, apart from writing and publishing a book that deserves them. My advice is to simply concentrate on writing and publishing a HIGH QUALITY book – if you do this, the positive reviews will follow naturally.

There are a number of different ways in which you can obtain fake or engineered reviews, but my advice is to steer well clear of these. For example, it is possible to pay for reviews on websites such as Fiverr.com. The main problem with this, apart from the fact that it is against Amazon's terms and conditions, is that your readers can see right through a fake or engineered review, and they may leave a comment on the review questioning its validity. Readers of your reviews also have the opportunity to 'VOTE' up or down the reviews your book receives, so if the readers of your review(s) find one of them to be particularly helpful, regardless of the fact of whether it's 1 star or 5 star, that review will go up to the top of the review rankings for your book. If it's a 1 star review they find the most helpful, sales of your book will literally dry up!

A few years back Amazon introduced something that is called the **AMAZON VERIFIED PURCHASE.** This was in direct response to many authors, publishers and general sellers of goods on Amazon complaining that too many people were leaving fake or engineered reviews on their products in an attempt to boost their sales and rakings.

When a product review is marked "Amazon Verified Purchase", it means that the customer who wrote the review actually purchased the item directly from Amazon. Customers can add this label to their review only if Amazon can verify that the item being reviewed was purchased at Amazon. Customers reading an **Amazon Verified Purchase** review can use this information to help them to decide which reviews are most helpful in their purchasing decisions.

If a review is not marked Amazon Verified Purchase, it doesn't mean that the reviewer has no experience with the product – it just means that Amazon couldn't verify that it had been purchased from Amazon. The customer may have purchased the item elsewhere or had another interaction with it. The Amazon Verified Purchase Review label offers one more way to help gauge the quality and relevance of a product review.

The whole point of me raising the AVP system on Amazon is to simply state the obvious – the more positive Amazon Verified Purchase reviews your book obtains on Amazon, the more likely it will sell better.

TIP: There is absolutely nothing wrong with you asking people within your network to buy your book direct from Amazon and then leave a review. It is important, however, to ask those people to provide a review that is both honest and genuine and based on their actual experiences of the book and how it helped them. You MUST NOT try to influence them in anyway. If they leave a poor review then you must use their comments to improve the book for the next print-run or revised edition.

Reasons why people leave poor reviews

Here are a number of reasons why people leave poor reviews on books, and how you can avoid them:

1. Poor formatting on the Kindle versions. When getting your book for-matted for Kindle be sure to use a reputable company, or some-one who at least knows what they are doing. The danger with trying to format your book yourself is that you are more likely to make a mistake, and the book will not read properly on the Kindle reading device. If there are errors with the formatting people will probably leave a poor review. Read the chapter on outsourcing to learn how to hire professionals that are capable of formatting your Kindle book.

2. Poor customer service or delivery issues. The good thing about this is that people who buy your book direct from Amazon will probably experience great customer service and fast delivery. If they buy your book direct from your own website or blog and the delivery is slow or customer service sub-standard, they may well head to Amazon to leave you a negative review. If selling a book from your own website, be sure to provide excellent customer service.

3. Mistakes, poor grammar, spelling and punctuation. If your book is riddled with errors then people will almost always leave a negative review. Of course, it is very difficult to write and publish a book that is totally error-free, and if there are just one or two slight issues with the content then most readers will forgive this. However, if it is clear to the reader that the author has made little or no effort to get the book checked, proofread or edited, then a negative review will be on its way to them toot-sweet!

To summarise, the only real way to gain fantastic reviews of your book is to write and publish great content that your readers will love.

POINT OF INTEREST 5: Your books ranking

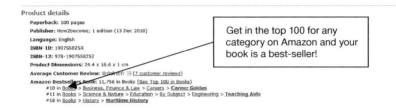

Product details

Paperback: 100 pages
Publisher: How2become; 1 edition (13 Dec 2010)
Language: English
ISBN-10: 190755825X
ISBN-13: 978-1907558252
Product Dimensions: 24.4 x 16.6 x 1 cm
Average Customer Review: ★★★★★ (7 customer reviews)
Amazon Bestsellers Rank: 11,756 in Books (See Top 100 in Books)
   #10 in Books > Business, Finance & Law > Careers > Career Guides
   #11 in Books > Science & Nature > Education > By Subject > Engineering > Teaching Aids
   #18 in Books > History > Maritime History

Get in the top 100 for any category on Amazon and your book is a best-seller!

Your books ranking will not generally have any impact on conversion rate, simply because your average customer will not be aware that the Amazon book rankings exist. To you, however, a book's ranking is very important. If your book manages to rank in the top 100 of any category on Amazon, you are automatically a best-seller, and this 'status' can be used to help promote your book.

Amazon's book rankings are not that easy to understand, and there do not seem to be many people who understand them outside of Amazon. However, from my own experience of selling on Amazon for a number of years, here's what I do know:

- Amazon's book rankings are updated every hour.

- If a customer purchases a book on Amazon it may not get registered as a sale on the book ranking system for a few hours.

- Amazon lists approximately 8 million books.

- If a book does not have any ranking, this means it hasn't sold any copies.

- If you see a book with a rank in the four or five million range, you'll know it's a poor seller.

- A book's rank will change hourly, unless it has not sold any copies. A book may gain a good rank due to a burst of sales, but if it doesn't sell any more after that it will gradually fall down the rankings.

- If your book reaches the top 100 of any book category then your book is classed as an Amazon best-seller. Each particular book is ranked against every book sold on Amazon. To put it simply, the smaller the number your book's rank is, the better, and if you have a ranking of 4,000, it means that 3,999 books are ahead of you in terms of book sales.

- In general, a ranking in the five digits, say 30,000, means your book is selling relatively well on Amazon. Many of my books consistently rank in the top 10,000 on Amazon, every hour of the day.

The following is not exact, however it will give you a rough indication as to how many books you might sell based on a particular ranking:

Amazon Bestseller-Rank	Estimated book sales per week
10,000	30
100,000	6
1,000,000	< 1

Disclaimer: The Amazon book ranking changes continuously, and therefore the information provided here is not guaranteed – it is simply a guide.

POINT OF INTEREST 6: Frequently bought together

Your book will sell better if listed with other books in the FREQUENTLY BOUGHT TOGETHER area of the Amazon sales-page.

Amazon is the master of the upsell! At every opportunity Amazon is trying to tempt you into buying additional items – this is great news for you as an author and self-publisher.

On the Amazon sales-page you will see the **FREQUENTLY BOUGHT TOGETHER** (FBT) options. These are books that have often been purchased in conjunction with the main item being listed on that particular page. You will notice that the FBT options are presented with a BUY NOW button, which says something like 'Add all three to basket'. The customer will also have the option to remove one or more of the additional FBT items listed based on their preferences. The aim of the game is to get your book listed with as many other books as possible in the FBT area of the sales-page. If you manage to achieve this, sales will increase significantly. If you can manage to get your book listed on the FBT section with another best-seller, you are onto a winner!

POINT OF INTEREST 7: Customers who bought this also bought

The more your book sells with other books, the further to the left it will appear on the 'Customers Who Bought This Also Bought' section.

This area of the Amazon sales-page works in conjunction with the FREQUENTLY BOUGHT TOGHETHER section. If one person buys your book along with another, you will automatically get listed in this section. The more times your book is purchased with a particular book the further to the left of the page your book will move, until eventually it makes its way up to the FREQUENTLY BOUGHT TOGETHER section. The problem is with some books is that there are many pages of 'Customers Who Bought This Also Bought', and therefore it could take some time before your book makes it along the pages and finally ends up in the FBT area for a particular book.

If you are like me and you intend writing and publishing a 'series' of books, then the aim is to get all of your own books on the first page of the 'Customers Who Bought This Also Bought', and also into the FBT section. You will see that on my ARMED FORCES TESTS book sales-page on the following page that every book featured on the 'Customers Who Bought This Also Bought' section and the FBT section belongs to me.

Nine of my books feature on the 1st page of the 'Customers Who Bought This Also Bought' section for this book. Your aim should be to get your book featuring on as many pages possible in this section.

POINT OF INTEREST 8: Your Amazon author page

The majority of authors selling their books on Amazon do not take the time to create an 'author page'. Whilst you do have the opportunity to add a description about the author when submitting your book to the Amazon Advantage programme, you will not be able to add a photo. In order to create a proper authors page you will need to sign up at the following link:

https://authorcentral.amazon.co.uk

Alternatively, simply search for 'Amazon Author Central' in Google and you will see the relevant page appear.

As an author it is very important that you set up your Amazon Authors page for the following reasons:

1. A dedicated author page will help you to build trust with your customers and readers.

2. If a customer can see the 'real' person behind the book, they are more likely to click the BUY NOW button.

3. When you set up your author page you will be able to add a photograph, a biography, a video, and also a link your twitter account (if you have one). Your Amazon author page will inform your customers of the latest 'tweets' you have made; therefore, it is important that you update your twitter feed regularly if you intend linking one to your authors page.

4. When you access your dedicated author's page you will be able to review your sales ranking statistics for all of your books (updated hourly). In addition to this, you will also be able to see any customer reviews and what people are saying about your books. This is particularly useful if you have lots of books on sale with Amazon. If you receive any negative reviews of your book(s) on Amazon then you may want to take the opportunity to inform the reviewer that you will take their feedback on-board and review the book for the next edition.

My Amazon Authors page

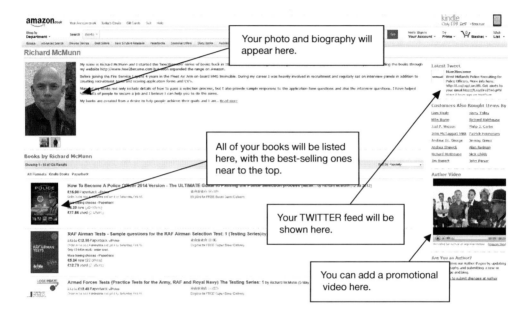

Sample author biography

To help you construct your own biography, you can take a read of my own one below:

My name is Richard McMunn, and I started the 'how2become' series of books back in 2005 when I was working as a Firefighter for Kent Fire & Rescue Service. I initially started selling the books through my website http://www.how2become.com but soon expanded the range on Amazon. Before joining the Fire Service I spent 4 years in the Fleet Air Arm on-board HMS Invincible. During my career I was heavily involved in recruitment, and regularly sat on interview panels in addition to creating recruitment tests and scoring application forms and CV's. Many of my books not only include details of how to pass a selection process, but I also provide sample responses to the application form questions and also the interview questions. I have helped hundreds of people to secure a job, and I believe I can help you to do the same. My books are created from a desire to help people achieve their goals, and I am sure you will find my books inspiring and motivational.

I hope you enjoy my books,

Richard McMunn

Tips for creating your author biography

1. Keep it relatively short. Between 150 and 200 words will be sufficient.

2. Write your biography as if you are speaking to the person reading it.

3. Try including the following in your biography:

- Who you are;

- Your experiences, qualifications and background;

- Why you decided to write your book(s);

- The aim of your book(s);

- How your book(s) will be of benefit to the reader.

Now that we have covered the key elements of the Amazon sales page, let's now move onto the different account options available to you in order to get your books listed and on sale.

During the next section of this chapter I will explain the different accounts you can use in order to sell your book(s) on Amazon. To begin with, I will explain the Amazon Advantage programme.

THE AMAZON ADVANTAGE PROGRAMME

Amazon Advantage is described by Amazon as "a simple, direct and profitable way to sell your items on the UK's leading online retailer."

Amazon Advantage is designed for authors, publishers, labels, and studios of all sizes to promote and sell their items on Amazon.co.uk. Whilst it is not exclusive to book publishers and book sellers, it is my preferred choice for selling my books on Amazon.

The benefits of the Amazon Advantage programme include:

- Amazon is, at the time of writing, the UK's number 1 online retailer.
- The website is open for business 24 hours a day, 7 days a week, and 365 days a year. Basically, you make money whilst you sleep!
- Unlike a traditional High Street book seller, there are no shelf space constraints.

Within the Amazon Advantage programme there are a number of different options available to you. I have listed these, including the payment percentages for books, below:

Advantage

Available Product Lines: Books, Music, DVD and Video

Discount Rates:

Books: 60% off List Price

Payment to Advantage Members:

Books: 40% of List Price

Advantage Premium [Subject to annual purchases > £50,000]

Available Product Lines: Books, Music, DVD and Video

Discount Rates:

Books: 55% off List Price

Payment to Advantage Members:

Books: 45% of List Price

Advantage Professional

Available Product Lines: Academic & Professional Books

Discount Rates:

Books: 40% off List Price

Payment to Advantage Members:

Books: 60% of List Price

Advantage Professional Premium [Subject to annual purchases > £25,000]

Available Product Lines: Academic & Professional Books

Discount Rates:

Books: 35% off List Price

Payment to Advantage Members:

Books: 65% of List Price

Regardless of the options listed, the following applies to each:

- Items have 'In stock' onsite availability

- There is no **upper** or **lower limit** of items being stocked

- There is an Annual Fee of £23.50 (including VAT)

- Sales & Inventory reports are available online 24/7, which can be managed from your account area.

My advice for authors and self-publishers, who want to publish their own books and sell them through a variety of different selling channels, including Amazon, would be to opt for the Advantage programme. To apply for an Amazon Advantage account, go to the following website:

http://advantage.amazon.co.uk/

The application process is relatively straightforward. However, if you have any issues when setting up your account you can contact Amazon directly at the HELP page, which is listed on their webpage.

How does Amazon place orders from you?

As customers order your items Amazon will monitor your inventory and automatically order more copies of a title when they get low on stock, and they will notify you via e-mail when you have a new order. The amount Amazon orders is based on the recent sales performance of your title. To learn more about Amazon's payment terms and conditions please see the relevant section on the Amazon Advantage website. Alternatively, if you would like personal support and guidance from me, please join my Book Publishing Academy at:

http://bookpublishingacademy.co.uk/

Frequently asked questions relating to Amazon Advantage

In this section I will try to answer some of the more common questions I get asked by authors and publishers with regards to the Amazon Advantage programme.

Q. Does Amazon print my books for me once I join the Amazon Advantage programme?

A. No. It is your responsibility to get your books printed yourself. You have to send Amazon the number of books they request when they submit a purchase order to you. For example, if they order 20 of a particular book from you you need to send that exact amount to them within a set period of time, as per their terms and conditions.

Q. Do I need an ISBN and bar code?

A. Yes you do. Your book will need to have an ISBN and bar code to be listed on the Amazon Advantage programme. The ISBN (International Standard Book Number) is a 13 digit number which is exclusive to your book – no other book will ever have the same number as yours. In order to submit a book to sell on the Amazon Advantage programme you MUST have both of these. You can obtain ISBN numbers from Nielsen Bookdata (www.isbn.nielsenbook.co.uk). With regards to the barcode, there are many companies who will charge you to create a bar code for you – this is not necessary. There is a piece of software which will create your barcode for you for free. You can download the software from:

http://www.nchsoftware.com/barcode/

The barcode, once generated with your own unique ISBN, will look something like this:

ISBN: 9781909229808

It is important that the ISBN is also included above the bar code. The bar-code and ISBN would normally be placed in the bottom right hand corner of the book.

Q. Once I have opened my Amazon Advantage account, how do I get my book uploaded?

A. Adding a book to the Amazon Advantage account is a relatively straight-forward process. You will need both the front book cover and your ISBN to get it active and on sale. Any item added to your account must have the ISBN printed on the back as well as a bar code that scans to this same ISBN. The reason for this is because the Amazon staff will scan your bar code at the depot when they receive your purchase orders.

Note: You cannot sell used items through the Advantage Programme. To sell used items, please visit **Amazon.co.uk Marketplace.**

Step 1: Once logged into your Amazon Advantage account select **'Book'** from the drop-down menu.

Step 2: Enter the 13 digit ISBN in the resulting entry window without dashes, then click **'Next'**.

Step 3: You will then be taken through to the book information page, where you will be asked to input the following fields, which are 'required' and 'optional' fields:

Amazon Advantage Required Fields

Book Title – enter the exact title of your book including sub-title. You are not permitted to use ALL capital letters. However, I usually enter one word in capitals which forms part of the sub-title. This will usually be an 'emotion' word such as ULTIMATE or DEFINITIVE. For example:

> How To Become A Firefighter: The ULTIMATE guide to passing the firefighter selection process 2014 version

Author – enter the name of the book's author here. You are permitted to enter more than one author if the book has been written in conjunction with others.

Publisher - enter the publisher. This will be the name of your publishing company or the business name from which the book has been published. If you are a sole trader then it is acceptable to enter your own name as the publisher – for example:

Richard McMunn Publishing

Publication Date – enter the date on which the book will be published. It is permissible to place your book on pre-order, even a year before it is released! I usually add my books to Amazon on pre-order many months before the anticipated publishing date. This enables your book to gain exposure and rankings before it is even launched.

Binding – enter the binding of your book. The majority of books I publish are a paperback binding.

Pages – enter the book's number of pages in this field. If it is yet to be published and you are unsure of the page length, simply enter the approximate page length and change it once you know the exact number.

Language – enter the language of the book here. At the time of writing the following language options are available to you:

English, German, French, Italian, Spanish, Danish, Hindi, Chinese, Japanese, Korean, Welsh, Other

Amazon Advantage Optional Fields

Subject – choose the subject category and sub-category here. Although this field is optional, I recommend that you choose a main subject category and sub-category. This will help your book to appear in Amazon search results.

Edition & Volume – enter the edition and volume number in these two fields. If this is the first publication of this particular book, enter the number 1 in each field.

Format – enter the format of your book in this field. At the time of writing you may choose from:

•Abridged

•Illustrated

•Large Print

•Box Set

•Audiobook

Description – enter the book's description here. You have 3,900 characters to create your description. Don't forget to read my useful tips on creating a book description. In order to add line breaks in your book description (applies to Amazon Advantage account only), insert the following code immediately after the full stop where you want the line break to begin:

**

**

Author Bio – enter the author's biography here. Again, you have 3,900 characters to use.

Editor – you may decide to enter the name of the book's editor in this field.

Amazon will also allow you to add additional contributors here such as the book's illustrator.

Review 1, 2 and 3 – you will have the option to enter up to 3 reviews for your book here. You can also add the source of the review(s). Book reviews will help to increase conversions, but the reviews must be genuine!

Q. Once Amazon place an order for my book(s), how do I acknowledge and dispatch the purchase order, and also, where do I send it to?

A. I will explain below and in detail what you need to do once you receive a purchase order from Amazon Advantage:

STEP 1

When Amazon wants to order books from you they will email you with a purchase order, very much like the one below:

--------Original Message--------

From: advantage-uk@amazon.co.uk. [mailto:advantage-uk@amazon.co.uk.]
Sent: 12 December 2013 14:52
To: dkguides4you@gmail.com
Cc: dkguides4you@gmail.com
Subject: You have an Amazon.co.uk Advantage order

Greetings from Amazon.co.uk Advantage !

You have a NEW order awaiting your confirmation: V5732581.

Account Name: Your Business Success Club Ltd
Your Advantage Vendor Code: YOVU7

Please record this number for future reference and note that this is a
NEW order and not a reminder for an earlier order.

Please confirm that you can fulfil this order as soon as possible by
visiting our site at htpp://www.amazon.co.uk/advantage
Once there, click the "Log-in" button to the left side of thr screen.
After entering your account e-mail address login and password to sign in,
click the Orders tab at the top of the page to access your Orders.
Click on the unconfirmed order. The subsequent screen will provide all
the quantity and shipping information you need to fulfil this order.

Please do not ship any copies until you have confirmed your order. Note
that we do expect to receive your books within one week of the order
date. Please ensure that we receive your shipment within this time
period. This will enable us to continue to honour the prompt
availability promise we make to customers ordering your title(s).

If you still have questions, please contact our Vendor Services team
using the "Contact Us" link located at the bottom of every page in
your Advantage account.

Sincerely,

The Advantage Team
Amazon.co.uk

*NOTE: It is very important that you CONFIRM & ACKNOWLEDGE the
purchase order within 24 hours.*

STEP 2

Once you receive the purchase order login to your Amazon Advantage
account.

STEP 3

The next step is to click on the Unconfirmed PO's link, which will take you through to the purchase order details.

STEP 4

Choose the DELIVERY DATE for your Purchase Order and click SAVE & CONFIRM.

STEP 5

Print off the ADDRESS LABEL and the PICKING SLIP. The address label will detail exactly which warehouse you are required to send your books to.

STEP 6

Now PRINT SHIPPING LABEL and also PRINT A PICK LIST

The SHIPPING LABEL should be attached to the outside of the jiffy bag or box that the book(s) are going to be sent to Amazon in. The PICK LIST should be placed inside the jiffy bag or box that the books are going to be sent in.

NOTES:

- Do not place sellotape over the bar code of the shipping label, as Amazon need to scan this when they receive the package at the other end. It is acceptable to place sellotape over the remainder of the SHIPPING LABEL, if you choose to do so.

- If the purchase order is large and you need to send more than one jiffy bag or box, place one SHIPPING LABEL on each jiffy bag or box, and also place one PICK LIST inside each jiffy bag or box.

WHAT TO SEND YOUR BOOKS IN

Personally, I send small orders in jiffy bags which I obtain from the following website:

www.davpack.co.uk

You can get up to 2 books in a size FLG1 jiffy bag.

You can get up to 4 books in a size FLG3 jiffy bag.

You can get between 6 and 8 books in a size FLG5 jiffy bag, depending on the size and thickness of your books.

For larger orders I pack the books in boxes, which I again purchase from DAVPACK.

I find that I can get up to 50 books in Davpack boxes, but I recommend that you wrap the box in plenty of brown sticky tape to protect it during its journey to Amazon. I usually order my brown sticky tape in bulk from **www.viking-direct.co.uk.**

HOW TO SEND YOUR BOOKS TO AMAZON

For the smaller jiffy bag orders, I send them by standard Royal Mail postage.

For the boxes, I send them by courier via the following website, which I have found to be very cost-effective:

www.parcelmonkey.com/

AMAZON CREATESPACE PROGRAMME

In this next section I will explain what I know about Amazon CreateSpace.

CreateSpace is a fantastic place to get your book self-published. The reason why I do not publish on this platform is simply because I want to have control of my stock, and I also want the ability to sell through multiple channels. CreateSpace is undoubtedly a brilliant place to sell your book, and there are benefits to this platform over Advantage. However, for me as a serious publisher I want to be able to have total control over all of my stock and my publishing strategy. So, in a nutshell, if you only intend publishing one book, and you only want to sell it on Amazon, seriously consider the CreateSpace programme.

Overview of CreateSpace

Amazon CreateSpace offers free tools and professional services to help make the entire publishing and distribution process cost-effective, fast, and easy-to-use. Printing, manufacturing and shipping is taken care of, so you do not have to order your own books from a 3rd party printer. Your book will remain in-stock and never run out. CreateSpace also offers you a free Interior Reviewer and Cover Creator, which also means you do not need to spend your own money on book cover design!

Some of the benefits to publishing on CreateSpace

- Book covers are printed in full-colour and laminated for durability
- Professional quality trade paperback binding
- Printed on white or cream paper
- Free ISBN will be supplied, if you do not already have one

CreateSpace royalties and the payment system

The royalty system with CreateSpace will depend on a number of factors, including:

- the trim size of your book (you can choose this yourself)

- the number of pages of your book

- interior type (black & white, full colour etc)

To give you an example, a 200 page book, printed in black & white with a trim size of 5" x 8" (industry standard), and with a retail price of £13 will give you a royalty of approximately £5.10 per unit sold. This is certainly comparable with royalties that I personally receive from a similar size and style of book through the Advantage programme. Although the royalty standards are different for each programme, I personally get excellent rates with my UK-based printer (per unit) which allows me to make more per book sale than your average book publisher.

You can sign up for a CreateSpace programme here:

www.createspace.com/

WHICH AMAZON PROGRAMME SHOULD I CHOOSE?

It certainly makes sense for those people who solely want to sell on Amazon to opt for the CreateSpace programme, simply because they will not have to pay for their own stocks of books, book cover design, typesetting costs, and shipping.

Books that are sold through the Advantage programme come from your own stock of books, however you will have the benefit of having lots of books in stock to sell to other channels, including your own blog or website. With Advantage you are going to have to pay for shipping the books to the Amazon Warehouse, so you need to account for additional money there in postage and packing material.

In general, books listed through CreateSpace will always be offered to the buying public at full price. When selling through the Advantage programme, since the discount is so high Amazon may offer your books at a 10%, 20% or even 30% discount, which makes it more attractive to the buyer. Your royalty rate through Advantage is based on list price, so if Amazon decides to discount your book you are still paid the same amount. Whether a discount is offered, it is at the sole discretion of Amazon and you have no control over this. It is actually to your benefit if they offer your book as a discount because you WILL sell more. I have found that on occasions I have listed books through the Advantage programme at £15, only for Amazon to sell it for less than £10! This works for me as I still get my royalty based on the £15 list price.

Conclusion

Amazon has some pretty steep fees associated with both programmes, but it is a beast and you cannot afford to NOT have your books listed on an Amazon sales-page. The good news is that it is remarkably easy to do, and they provide some very flexible alternatives for self-published authors.

CHAPTER 9
SELLING THROUGH MULTIPLE CHANNELS

Get instant access to over 32 hours' worth of online training videos and support at:

www.BookPublishingAcademy.co.uk

SELLING THROUGH MULTIPLE CHANNELS

I have always said that one of the main reasons for my success in publishing is because I sell through multiple channels.

Within this section of the book I will explain what this means, and how you can also get your book under the noses of many different booksellers. The first thing to stress, however, is that in order to sell your physical books through many different channels you will need to hold your own stock. The problem with holding onto lots of physical stock is that you need the space to achieve this, and this can cost you in terms of business rates for the extra square footage required. However, if you opt for digital printing you will be able to keep sufficient stock to meet demand without having to pay for expensive storage or office space. One other cute method to employ is to actually ask your printer to ship your digital titles direct to your main distributors. You can obtain quotes for digital printing from me at **www.BookPublishingAcademy.co.uk.**

At the time of writing I sell both physical and digital books to a variety of different book buyers, including Gardners.com, WHSmiths, Waterstones, eBay, independent book stores and hundreds of UK book sellers.

Making use of a distributer to sell through multiple channels (Garnders)

A book distributer is an organisation who will stock your books on consignment basis and sell them to literally thousands of book retailers around the globe. The main reason why I choose to use a distributor is simply because I don't want the hassle and expense of having to make contact with all of the book retailers myself. Whilst there are a few other book distributors across the UK, I personally choose Gardners.com.

Gardners Books is 'Britain's Leading Book Wholesaler', and the supplier of choice for thousands of booksellers and retailers around the world. As a publisher you can take advantage of this by stocking or listing your titles with them. Gardners provides a one-stop shop for any book retailer, with the widest range of stock titles available in the UK. For you as the publisher, this provides you with instant access to over 15,000 retailers across the UK and overseas. Hopefully you can now see why I choose the Amazon Advantage programme as opposed to CreateSpace.

Whilst Gardners do take a large cut (negotiable), I have always found them extremely efficient, helpful and conscientious. In a nutshell, whenever I publish a new book I will send Gardners an **Advanced Trade Information** sheet (ATI), which will also include an image of the book cover. They will then upload the details of the book onto their system so that book retailers can order them direct from Gardners. When a book retailer orders stock direct from Gardners, Gardners will send the books direct to them based on minimum order levels. The retailer will then sell the books for a profit. In order to stock your books with Gardners.com you will need to apply for a publishers account.

How to get your books stocked with Gardners

The set of criteria you must meet in order to get your books stocked is as follows:

1) All publishers must be registered with Nielsen Bookdata. You can register here:

Website: www.nielsenbookdata.co.uk/

2) All books must have a valid ISBN and a visible barcode (most commonly on the bottom right of the back cover). You can find out more about obtaining ISBN numbers here:

www.isbn.nielsenbookdata.co.uk

Email : isbn@nielsenbookdata.co.uk

As previously covered, you can download a free bar code generator software tool at:

www.nchsoftware.com/barcode/

3) For stock titles the publisher must have UK Representation, and the stock must be available from a UK location. It is acceptable for yourself, as the publisher, to be the representative providing your stock is located in the UK.

4) To qualify as a stock line printed books must be available.

If your title(s) do meet the above criteria you will then need to send Gardners a sample copy for review to the following address, ensuring that they are clearly labelled as 'samples'. Please note: Gardners will not return samples or acknowledge receipt.

FAO Buyers New Publishers,

Buying Office,

Gardners Books,

1 Whittle Drive,

Eastbourne,

East Sussex

BN23 6QH.

What Happens Next?

Gardners will contact you if they decide to stock your books. Where it is agreed to stock books Gardners will then discuss commercial terms with you as the publisher. Almost without exception, books from new publisher relationships will be taken into stock on a consignment basis (i.e. they hold stock and pay monthly on sales achieved). Other commercial terms (e.g. discount levels) will also be agreed.

If you have not heard from Gardners within four weeks, this will mean they have decided not to hold your books in stock at this time. One way to improve your chances of Gardners taking on your books is to provide them with any previous sales records. For example, when I first approached Gardners to sell my books for me I sent them an entire six months sales sheets from sales generated both on Amazon and through my own website. I also offered to give them 60% discount off the recommend list price – I am sure this helped with their decision to stock my books.

NB. As a general rule of thumb: all books that are held as stock lines are 'sold' to the retail customer on a 'Sale or Return' basis.

Advanced Trade Information sheets

Advance Trade Information Sheets (ATI's), or simply AI's, should be sent four months before each title is produced, and they should be supplied by the publisher to the wholesaler and sales representatives, key accounts, overseas agents, and anyone else in the trade who might be interested in the book.

The ATI should normally contain the following:

- publisher's logo
- name of author(s), editor, illustrator, as appropriate
- title and sub-title, and series title where relevant
- publication date

- suggested retail price
- ISBN
- number of pages and illustrations
- format and binding(s)
- language
- two or three key selling points
- brief summary of contents, indicating localities where relevant
- brief details of the author(s) or editor: including where they are from and where they live
- intended readership
- promotional details: serialisation, press, TV & radio features, launches, etc
- reviews and recommendations: brief quotations from respected, named sources
- cover, author photograph or other appropriate image
- publisher's contact details
- distributors' contact details

Here is a sample ATI to give you a better idea of what one looks like:

SAMPLE ADVANCED TRADE INFORMATION SHEET

Suite 3, 50 Churchill Square, Kings Hill, Kent. ME19 4YU
Mobile No. 07890 183 416
Contact Email Address   info@how2become.co.uk
Publishers Website Address www.how2become.com

(Jacket Illustration)

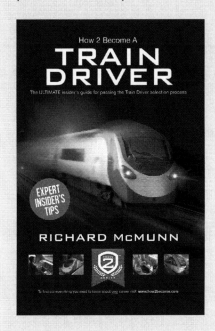

Title: How To Become A Train Driver: the insider's guide
ISBN 9781909229501
Author/Illustrator- Richard McMunn
Size in mm - 19.4 x 12.8 x 10 mm
Pages -160
Binding - Paperback
Age – Adult
Publication Date – 14th January 2014

SYNOPSIS:

HOW TO BECOME A TRAIN DRIVER: THE INSIDER'S GUIDE

Want to become a Train Driver? There are more candidates than ever, but
this INSIDER'S guide will help you get the career you want. The selection
process for becoming a Train Driver includes a requirement to complete an

application form, attend an assessment day, and pass two interviews.

This comprehensive guide will take you through the entire selection process and help you to secure this fantastic career at the first attempt. The selection process is highly competitive, but there a number of things you can do in order to increase your chances of success.

This guide contains:

- Tips on completing a successful application;
- Sample responses to the application form questions;
- Tips on how to prepare for the assessment day;
- Sample Group Bourdon/Concentration tests;
- Sample Trainibility for Rules and Procedures Test;
- Advice on the new train driver tests and how to pass them;
- Insider tips on how to pass the interviews;
- Sample interview questions;
- Responses to the interview questions to help you prepare.

KEY SALES POINTS:

• Contains insider tips and advice from industry experts
• Provides sample interview questions and responses
• Provides advice for passing the NEW train driver tests
• Lots of sample testing questions

Richard McMunn is a former serving Fire Officer and now founder, creator and owner of the How2become.com careers website.

How2become.com is the UK's leading careers information website. We go to great lengths to find the right people to create our products. Sometimes, we even put a member of our team through a particular selection process so that we can find out exactly what it takes to pass. Visit www.how2become. com for more guides, products and training courses to help you succeed.

DISTRIBUTED BY: How2become Ltd

Distributors full address: Suite 3, 50 Churchill Square, Kings Hill, Kent. ME19 4YU
RRP: £13.00

Contact: How2become Ltd
Telephone No: 07890 XXX XXX
Email address: info@how2become.co.uk
Website address: www.how2become.com

NOTE: If you would like to download a copy of my sample ATI sheets to use within your publishing business, please join my Book Publishing Academy at www.BookPublishingAcademy.co.uk

Getting your book into Waterstones and other High Street stores

Waterstones buy all their books from small publishers via Gardners. Therefore, in order to get your book(s) listed in Waterstones, both online and in store, you will need to apply for an account. In order to sell to the Waterstones branches it is necessary to register with Waterstones via Gardners. To do this you will need to contact the **Independent Publisher Coordinator** by email: ipc@waterstones.com and ask for a 'Waterstones Trading Application Form'.

Once the form is completed you then need to return the form to Gardners, as explained on the form. Once you are registered Waterstones will notify you that you may market your books to their branches. Submitting the **Waterstones Trading Application Form** does not guarantee that Gardners will hold your stock.

When a branch of Waterstones orders copies of your books the orders go direct to Gardners, who in turn order from you or your distributor. The book is then delivered to Gardners, who will finally supply the branches. You will then invoice Gardners, who in turn will invoice Waterstones.

IMPORTANT NOTE: Waterstones will not accept deliveries direct to store, they must come via Gardners Books.

My view on selling your books through Waterstones

Purely from a business perspective, I do not put much effort into selling my books in Waterstones stores. Not only do my books sell far better on Amazon, but I have also found Waterstones difficult to deal with on occasions. This may simply be down to the fact that Waterstones cannot compete with Amazon prices in my particular niche area of careers related books.

My advice would certainly be to try and get your books on sale in Waterstones stores; after all, every additional sale is worth the effort! Please be aware that all the marketing for your book will be down to you, the publisher.

FAQ's relating to Waterstones

Q. Why do I have to fill out a form if I already have a trade account with Gardners?

A. Waterstones asked Gardners to ensure that publishers fill out the forms so that they have the correct data. They then use this data to ensure Nielsen Booknet Teleordering is sending the orders to the right place.

Q. What discount do I need to offer Waterstones?

A. New publishers are generally asked to give Gardners a minimum of 60% discount. You can offer less than that, but if the discount you offer reduces Waterstones and other retailers are less likely to support your book.

Q. Can I deliver my books direct to the store?

A. No. Waterstones insist that Gardners deliver the books, along with the electronic invoice and delivery note they need, to ensure you get paid. The good news is that Gardners will generally get the books to the Waterstones branch within 48 hours.

Selling on eBay

I recommend you sell your printed book on ebay, simply because this is a great additional selling channel to gain extra sales and exposure. If you intend stocking your books with Gardners.com, you will automatically be making your books available to thousands of UK book-sellers. For example, at the time of writing 349 book-sellers are listing my books for sale on eBay. This will include both new and second-hand. The way I see it, if there are 349 people willing to sell my books for me on eBay, there is absolutely no need for me to list them, too.

Most of the book-sellers who sell my books on eBay will buy them in advance from Gardners and then sell them on to make a profit; therefore, I will get the sale commission for these books as Gardners have already sold them. There will also be a number of book-sellers who simply list my books on eBay and then buy them from Gardners once they sell a copy. These book-sellers will usually offer buyers a cheaper price, but with extended delivery times.

Of course, you may decide to sell your books yourself through eBay. If you wish to follow this route, you can open your account at:

www.ebay.co.uk

CHAPTER 10
KINDLE AND EBOOKS

Get instant access to over 32 hours' worth of online training videos and support at:

www.BookPublishingAcademy.co.uk

KINDLE AND EBOOKS

Electronic book publishing, particularly on Amazon Kindle, has literally taken the publishing world by storm. Whilst many UK-based publishers rue the fact that Amazon dominates this rapidly expanding market, many writers and authors across the world are seeing handsome returns for their writing efforts. The fact that writers like you are now getting rewarded appropriately for their writing skills is, in my opinion, long overdue.

For too long writers received very low royalty rates for their work; however, the introduction of the Amazon Kindle back in 2007 levelled the playing field, which meant one thing for authors across the world - more profits and greater exposure for their book.

Publishing on the **Amazon Kindle Digital Text Platform** is a fast and effi-cient way to get your book in front of literally millions of readers worldwide. Here are just a few benefits of publishing your book on the Kindle:

- No face-to-face selling or having to deal with customer service/fulfilment.
- Amazon will electronically deliver the eBook for you.
- There are NO customer emails to deal with.
- Amazon has millions of customers worldwide (approximately

80,000,000 per month). Publish your book once and it will reach a global market.

- There are no set up fees to start selling your book on the Kindle.
- The Amazon Digital Text Platform has a fast set-up process. Publishing takes less than 5 minutes. Your book appears on Amazon within 24 hours.
- Amazon is a '24/7 – 365 days a year' operation which means your book sells whilst you sleep.
- You get very good support from Amazon.
- You still have the option to upsell within a Kindle book.
- You get to keep control, and you can make changes to your book at any time.
- You can earn a 70% royalty on every book you sell. This option is available to customers in the UK, US, Canada, Germany, India, France, Italy, Spain, Japan, Brazil, Mexico, and a few others.
- You are able to publish in multiple languages. You can publish in English, German, French, Spanish, Portuguese, Italian, and Japanese.

Kindle Direct Publishing Select (KDP Select)

Amazon has introduced what is called the KDP Select Global Fund. A share of this fund is available to authors and publishers who allow other people to read their book for free. As of January 2014 the Global Fund was a staggering $1.2 Million. Every time a reader borrows your book from the **Kindle Owners' Lending Library**, you will earn a share of the Global Fund.

What is the Kindle Owners' Lending Library?

The Kindle Owners' Lending Library is a collection of books that Amazon Prime members who own a Kindle can borrow once a month for no fee. Your books will still be available for anyone to buy in the Kindle Store, and you'll continue to earn royalties from those sales like you normally would.

What does it mean to publish exclusively on Kindle?

When you choose to enrol your book in KDP Select you're committing to make the digital format of that book available exclusively through KDP. During the period of exclusivity you cannot distribute your book digitally anywhere else, including on your website, blogs, etc. However, you can continue to distribute your book in physical format, or in any format other than digital.

From a personal perspective, I have found the KDP select worth enrolling in as my royalties have increased for Kindle books that are part of the programme – the only real issue for you is that you won't be able to sell the Kindle book anywhere else, not even on your own website.

TIP: You can still promote your book on your website, but you will need to link through to the Amazon sales page that your Kindle book is available to buy from.

HOW TO GET YOUR BOOK READY TO SELL ON KINDLE

In order to sell your book on the Amazon Kindle DTP you will need:

1. Your manuscript converted to a suitable format for Kindle.
2. The front cover of your book in JPEG format. JPEG, or JPG, is a common term used for a common file format for digital photos and other digital graphics.
3. An Amazon Kindle DTP account.

Let's take a look at each area individually.

Converting your manuscript for Kindle

There are many companies and individuals online who will offer to format your book for Kindle, and my advice is to use one of them providing they are professional and good at what they do.

Most people try to convert their book themselves using free online Kindle conversion software tools or by following Amazon's advice and free step-by-step guide on how to do it yourself. Whilst these tools do work, they will usually always leave formatting errors within the book. My advice is to employ the services of an outsourcer to format your book for you.

The great thing about Kindle, from a customer/readers perspective, is that Amazon offers a 7-day money back guarantee on Kindle eBooks. Here's what Amazon says on their website about refunds:

"Books you purchase from the Kindle Store are eligible for return and refund if we receive your request within 7 days of the date of purchase. Once a refund is issued, you will no longer have access to the book."

One of the most important aspects of publishing on Kindle is to give no reason for your customers to request a refund. Regardless of how good your content is, if you mess up with the formatting, customers WILL request a refund. What's even worse, they will most probably then also leave a negative review on your book – and we all know what impact a negative review can have on our books!

My advice would be to get the book formatted by a professional individual or organisations. Personally, I use ODesk.com to get my books converted, and I usually pay approximately $100-$150 for a book which contains approximately 150-200 pages. The cost for conversion when using ODesk.com will very much depend on the complexity of the book. For example, if there are lots of images or charts within the content then this will increase the price. Before you go ahead and hire a professional outsourcer to format your book please make sure you read the relevant chapter on outsourcing, as it will help you to avoid the common pitfalls.

I have, on occasions, used UK-based companies to format my Kindle books, but they are usually a lot more expensive. If you do wish to pay a little more for your formatting, I recommend the following UK company:

www.fingerpress.co.uk

You will need to send the individual or company both your completed manuscript (preferably in Word) and the front book cover image in JPEG format. For Kindle conversion you do not need to get the full book cover jacket created with spine and rear text. You also do not need to add the ISBN or bar code to the cover; just the front book cover will be fine.

If you do want to have a try at formatting your own book for Kindle please go to the following page, and in particular the HELP section:

https://kdp.amazon.com

There is a useful forum on this site where you can ask questions relating to formatting, uploading, and selling your book(s) on Kindle. There are also step-by-step guides you may want to read which have been published by Amazon on how to get your book published on Kindle – just search on Amazon.co.uk for **'Publish on Amazon Kindle with Kindle Direct Publishing'**, and **'Building Your Book for Kindle'** - you can download these books for free.

Compatible format types accepted by Amazon

Kindle Direct Publishing (KDP) lets you upload and convert your final draft from several formats. For best results, Amazon recommends that you upload in DOC/DOCX (.doc/.docx) or HTML (.html) format. However, from personal experience I have always formatted my book in ePub. The reason for this is that the Apple iBookStore and Gardners eWarehouse will only accept eBooks in ePub format. Therefore, in order to save on cost it is advisable to get your book formatted in ePub, and you can then sell it through multiple channels.

Here is the full list of formats accepted by Amazon DTP:

- Word (DOC or DOCX)
- HTML (ZIP, HTM, or HTML)
- MOBI (MOBI)
- ePub (EPUB)
- Rich Text Format (RTF)
- Plain Text (TXT)
- Adobe PDF (PDF)

Using the Amazon Kindle Book Cover Creator

Amazon provides a free book cover creator. I have used it on a number of occasions, and whilst the quality is not as good as using a professional designer it is a great way to get started if your budget is low.

In order to use the Kindle Cover Creator, click on the "Add new title" button once you are signed into your account. Next, click "Design with Cover Creator" in section 4, then "Upload Your Cover." The Cover Creator interface will automatically launch and instructions will then be provided on how to create your cover.

As I have already mentioned on numerous occasions, the image you use for your cover will be the first thing people will see when they find your book, so choose an image that really represents the quality and subject of your book. You can provide your own image or select from the gallery of stock images available.

Images you provide should be of high quality, and you must hold all rights necessary to use the image for your book cover. See the chapter relating to Book cover designs and book titles for more tips on how create a fantastic book cover.

Choosing a Design

After you've uploaded or selected your image you can choose from one of ten base designs, which can then be further customised with various layouts as well as font and colour schemes. In case you can't find an image you're satisfied with, Amazon has included some basic designs that don't incorporate an image from your computer or the stock image gallery.

Customising your layout

Once you've selected a base design you can choose from an assortment of font sets, colour schemes, and text layouts or make changes to your text and images directly by clicking on each part.

Previewing and submitting your cover

When you have completed designing your cover, click the "Preview Cover" button to check how it looks in colour, grayscale, and thumbnail modes.

Once you're satisfied with your cover, click "Save & Submit" to submit your cover to KDP. Cover Creator will close and your cover will be loaded in the "Edit book details" page of KDP.

Getting paid by Amazon for Kindle sales

Separate royalty payments for each Kindle Store in which you have chosen to distribute your title will be paid automatically by Electronic Funds Transfer (EFT), Wire Transfer (where available), or cheque approximately sixty (60) days following the end of the calendar month during which applicable sales occur once the threshold is met. Keep in mind that your bank may charge fees for some payments. If you're not sure whether they do, you may want to contact them.

How to see how many Kindle books you have sold

In your Amazon KDP account there are a number of reports available for you to view at any time, and these are listed as follows:

Month-to-Date Unit Sales

You can use this report to get a quick snapshot of your unit sales and transactions for the current month's sales.

Prior Six Weeks' Royalties

This report shows transactions and royalties you've earned over the six weeks prior to the current week.

Prior Months' Royalties

These reports show summaries of previous months' sales transactions, for the last 12 months. Reports are generated near the 15th day of each month and include sales that occurred within the prior month.

HOW TO UPLOAD YOUR BOOK TO THE AMAZON KINDLE DIGITAL TEXT PLATFORM, PLUS USEFUL TIPS

In this section of the chapter I will show you how to upload a book to your Amazon Kindle Digital text Platform.

STEP 1 – Open your account

In order to open your account, please go to:

https://kdp.amazon.com/

STEP 2 – Add new title

Once you have signed up for your account and logged in, please now click the ADD NEW TITLE button which is located in the top left hand corner of the dashboard.

STEP 3 – Consider choosing Kindle Select

One of the first decisions you will need to make when you come to upload your eBook to your account area is whether or not to enrol your book onto Kindle select.

If you decide to include your eBook in Kindle Select you are enrolling for 90 days, during which time your eBook must not be available in digital format on any other platform. If your book is found to be available elsewhere in digital format it may not be eligible to remain in the program.

The decision on whether to include your book in KDP Select is entirely yours. As previously mentioned, the programme has been beneficial for me.

STEP 4 – Enter your book's details

In the next section of your account area you will need to add the details of your book.

- Book name

Taking what you have learnt so far, input the name of your book in this field. You just need to input the main title of your book, and not the subtitle or strapline.

- Subtitle (optional)

The subtitle is your book's strapline. Although it says 'optional' my advice would be to insert one, especially if your genre falls into anything outside of fiction. A subtitle will be picked up in the search engines, which may help with conversions.

- This book part of a series

If your book is part of a series, insert it here. For example, my books fall under the 'how2become' series. Once your brand becomes established and readers learn to love your books, they will start to search for your brand or series of books. If you intend publishing more than one book, consider having a series name.

- Edition number (optional)

Providing the version number can help readers to know whether the book is the original edition or if it contains updated content. If this is the first time you have published this book, enter the numeral 1. If the book was previously published and the version you are publishing contains significant changes, enter the numeral 2 (and so on).

- Publisher (optional)

Because you will be the author and publisher of your book, you can enter your name or the name of your publishing company here.

- Description

Your book description is what customers see as they shop in the Kindle store. If you are publishing a printed version too, the description should be the same. Within the description I recommend you consider including the main title of the book 2-3 times. This will help your book to rank in the search results. Here is a sample book description to help you:

How to become a police officer - The ULTIMATE Guide to Passing the Police Selection process (NEW Competencies) is the most up-to-date guide available for anyone wishing to become a police officer in the UK.

The guide has been written in conjunction with current serving police officers to bring you the very latest recruitment tips and advice based on the new core competencies, which include serving the public, openness to change, service delivery, public service, professionalism, decision making, and working with others.

The how to become a police officer book for aspiring police officers includes tips on passing the application form (including sample responses), competency based interview questions, role play and interactive exercises, the new tests, report writing, and there is even a section on the police final interview.

If you are SERIOUS about becoming a police officer then this is the only guide you will need.

You will notice that I have included the main title of the book on 2 occasions within the description, which will help the book to rank in the search engine results. Be careful not to include the main title of the book more than 2-3 times as the major search engine's may penalise you for what is commonly known as 'keyword stuffing'.

- Book contributors

Contributors are the people who have helped you to create your book. Within this field you can add and identify your book's author, editor, illustrator, translator, and more. If the book has more than one author, you can enter multiple authors. Enter author names in the sequence you would like them to appear in the Kindle store. To publish your book at least one contributor name is required. The first person you should add as a contributor is yourself as the 'author'.

- Language

In this field input the primary language in which the book has been written.

- Publication date (optional)

This is the date that you are publishing the guide. Simply leave it blank or select the date that you are publishing your eBook. Alternatively, if you already have the same book published in print-format select the date that the physical version was published.

TIP: Selecting a publication date will inform customers of how up-to-date your book is – this will help with conversion.

- ISBN (optional)

As previously stated, the ISBN is an International Standard Book Number. You do not need to have an ISBN to publish your Kindle book, but if you do have one enter it in this section. Do not use the same ISBN from a print edition for your digital edition. If you want to include an ISBN for the digital version of your book it must be a unique ISBN. You can purchase an ISBN from multiple sources on the Web, including the official ISBN body, Nielsen.

www.isbn.nielsenbook.co.uk/

- Verify your publishing rights

'Publishing rights' are the rights you need to have in order to publish a book. To publish a book for Kindle through KDP you must have obtained all rights necessary to publish the digital book from the book's author and any other content creators, or, if you are the book's author, you must have retained all of the necessary digital book publishing rights. If you are both the author and publisher, as is the case for most of my books, you will automatically have the rights.

If the book is your own and you hold the necessary rights for the content, select "This is not a public domain work and I hold the necessary publishing rights."

- Target your book to customers

There are many different categories on Amazon for your book to fall under, and in this section you will have the opportunity to select up to 2. In order to select the correct category, simply put yourself in the shoes of your readers. Which category would they need to search under in order to find your book? For example, my 'how2become' books always fall under the category of careers. At the time of writing, the following main 'non-fiction' categories are available on Kindle, each with additional sub-headings:

- ANTIQUES & COLLECTIBLES
- ARCHITECTURE
- ART
- BIBLES
- BIOGRAPHY & AUTOBIOGRAPHY
- BODY, MIND & SPIRIT
- BUSINESS & ECONOMICS
- COMICS & GRAPHIC NOVELS
- COMPUTERS
- COOKING
- CRAFTS & HOBBIES
- DESIGN
- DRAMA
- EDUCATION
- FAMILY & RELATIONSHIPS
- FICTION
- FOREIGN LANGUAGE STUDY
- GAMES
- GARDENING
- HEALTH & FITNESS
- HISTORY
- HOUSE & HOME
- HUMOR
- JUVENILE FICTION
- JUVENILE NONFICTION
- LANGUAGE ARTS & DISCIPLINES
- LAW

- LITERARY COLLECTIONS
- LITERARY CRITICISM
- MATHEMATICS
- MEDICAL
- MUSIC
- NATURE
- PERFORMING ARTS
- PETS
- PHILOSOPHY
- PHOTOGRAPHY
- POETRY
- POLITICAL SCIENCE
- PSYCHOLOGY
- REFERENCE
- RELIGION
- SCIENCE
- SELF-HELP
- SOCIAL SCIENCE
- SPORTS & RECREATION
- STUDY AIDS
- TECHNOLOGY & ENGINEERING
- TRANSPORTATION
- TRAVEL
- TRUE CRIME
- NON-CLASSIFIABLE

There are also the following fiction categories, each with sub-headings, too:

- FICTION
- JUVENILE FICTION

- Search keywords (up to 7, optional)

When you add keywords, these will help your readers to find your book when they search the Kindle Store. You can enter keywords or short phrases that describe your book and are relevant to its content. The best keywords are those that do not repeat words in the title, category, or description, as these are currently already used to help readers find your book. Please note: Amazon does not accept search keywords that mislead or manipulate their customers. Examples of items that are prohibited as search keywords include but are not limited to:

- Reference to other authors
- Reference to books by other authors
- Reference to sales rank (i.e. 'best-selling')
- Reference to advertisements or promotions (i.e. 'free')
- Reference to anything that is unrelated to your book's content

To give you an idea of the type of keywords I might include for a particular book, here is the main title and the keywords I would choose:

TITLE: How to Become a Firefighter

Keywords: Careers, interview questions, application forms, job hunting, psychometric tests, CV.

- Upload or create a book cover

This is the section where you get to upload the all-important book cover! Kindle Direct Publishing accepts only two types of files for cover images:

JPEG, or .jpeg

TIFF, or .tif(f)

KDP applies additional compression to images when displaying them on its website. For best results images should be uploaded with minimal compression.

Dimensions

Requirements for the size of your cover art have an ideal height/width ratio of 1.6, this means:

- A minimum of 625 pixels on the shortest side and 1000 pixels on the longest side
- For best quality your image would be 1563 pixels on the shortest side and 2500 pixels on the longest side

Colour

Product images display on the Amazon website using RGB (red, green, blue) colour mode. Use colour images whenever possible and relevant. The Kindle reading device has a black and white screen today, but Kindle applications for other devices such as iPhone or PC, take advantage of colour fonts and images.

Borders for White Cover Art

Cover art with white or very light backgrounds can seem to disappear against the white background. Adding a very narrow (3-4 pixel) border in medium gray will define the boundaries of the cover.

Uploading Your Cover

1. Log in: http://kdp.amazon.com/.

2. On your bookshelf, in the "Other Book Actions" column next to the title you're updating, click "Edit book details."

3. Scroll down to "Product Image."

4. Click "Browse for Image..."

5. A pop-up window will appear. Click "Browse."

6. Locate your cover image file on your computer, and click "Open."

7. Click the "Upload Image" button.

8. Uploaded Successfully! will appear, along with the preview image.

9. Scroll to the bottom of the page and click "Save and Continue."

STEP 5 - Upload Your Book File

During this next stage you will need to upload your formatted guide in either ePub or any other compatible format you have chosen. You will also have the option to select which level of Digital Rights Management (DRM) you want the guide to available under.

DRM is intended to inhibit unauthorised distribution of the Kindle file of your book. Some authors want to encourage readers to share their work, and choose not to have DRM applied to their book. If you choose DRM, customers will still be able to lend the book to another user for a short period, and can also purchase the book as a gift for another user from the Kindle store. Important: Once you publish your book, you cannot change its DRM setting.

STEP 6 - Preview Your Book

Once your formatted file has been uploaded you will have the chance to preview your book. Previewing your book is an integral part of the publishing process and the best way to guarantee that your readers will have a good experience and see the book you want them to see.

STEP 7 - Verify Your Publishing Territories

During step 7 you will verify your rights to publish the written work. As a self-publisher you will need to select **Worldwide rights – all territories.**

STEP 8 - Choose Your Royalty

You can choose between two royalty options: a 70% royalty option and a 35% royalty option. For example, for sales in the US, if your book's list price is between $2.99 and $9.99, you can choose the 70% option. The 35% option is available in the US for books with list prices between $.99 and $200.00. For the UK price setting based on a 70% royalty rate your book price must be between £1.49 and £7.81.

STEP 9 - Kindle MatchBook

Amazon states that the Kindle MatchBook program gives customers who purchase or have previously purchased your print book from Amazon the option to purchase your Kindle version for $2.99 or less. If you have a print version of this title, enrol your title and select a Promotional List Price that is lower than your Kindle List Price by at least 50%.

STEP 10 - Kindle Book Lending

Enrolment in Kindle Book Lending will allow users to lend your book after purchasing to their friends and family for a duration of 14 days.

Once you have followed all of the above 10 steps you are now ready to SAVE & PUBLISH your work. It usually takes no longer than 24-48 hours for your book to be visible and on sale through the Amazon Digital Text Platform.

Now let's move on and take a look at the important subject of how to protect your copyright and intellectual property.

CHAPTER 11

HOW TO PROTECT YOUR COPYRIGHT AND INTELLECTUAL PROPERTY

Get instant access to over 32 hours' worth of online training videos and support at:

www.BookPublishingAcademy.co.uk

HOW TO PROTECT YOUR COPYRIGHT AND INTELLECTUAL PROPERTY

One of the first and most important rules as an author and self-publisher is to protect your intellectual property.

As an author and self-publisher you will constantly be watching your competitors and trying to close the door on any 'holes in your business' that people could potentially exploit. For example, when I started writing my first book under the brand name 'how2become' I immediately looked at ways to protect the name. I felt it was a strong/unique name, and therefore I wanted to protect it. Using some of the early profits I was making from selling my guides I decided to apply for the trademark 'how2become'. It took me many months to get the trademark, but it was a very wise move.

Whilst obtaining a trademark can be a lengthy and expensive process, it is certainly worth the effort and the additional cost, especially if you have a good, strong brand or idea. The **National Business Register** is an excellent source for protecting your business name against 'passing off' and other common problems.

VISIT: www.start.biz

You will also want to protect your intellectual property by way of copyright. The purpose of copyright is to allow creators (authors) to gain economic rewards for their efforts, and so encourage future creativity and the development of new material, which benefits us all. Copyright material is usually the result of creative skill and/or significant labour and/or investment, and without protection it would often be very easy for others to exploit material without paying the creator. There is no official registration system for copyright in the UK and most other parts of the world, as registration is not needed.

There are no forms to fill in and no fees to pay to get copyright protection, as under a number of international conventions it is automatically granted to the creator of a copyrightable work. This means that as soon as you create a work which falls into one of the categories of material that qualifies for copyright protection, you will have copyright without having to do anything further to establish your claim.

However, copyright owners (authors) can take certain precautions to help establish their rights. A copy of your work could be deposited with a bank or solicitor. Alternatively, an author could send himself or herself a copy of their manuscript by special delivery post (which gives a clear date stamp on the envelope), leaving the envelope unopened on its return. You may also decide to simply email your manuscript to yourself by way of an attachment – this will provide proof that you actually own the rights to work on the date the email was sent. If you feel that it will take you many months or even years to finish your manuscript, simply send yourself each chapter as and when it is completed.

Whatever you do, make sure you take the time to protect your business environment and your intellectual property. You can find free and impartial advice with regard to copyright law, trademarks and patents at the following website:

www.ipo.gov.uk

There are many companies and solicitors out there that will charge you a considerable fee to protect your copyright. Whilst there is nothing wrong with taking this approach (providing you have the funds available), my advice would be to simply protect your IP for free using one of the methods described earlier in this section.

Non-disclosure and confidentiality agreements

Think very carefully about disclosing your book idea to others before you have obtained protection for it. Disclosure can also invalidate your ability to apply for protection. In many cases a third party will agree to sign a non-disclosure or confidentiality agreement (NDA). For example, whenever I coach my students during my one-to-one coaching programme at **www. RichardmentorMe.com**, I will always sign an NDA if the client asks me to.

If you have to disclose your idea, talk to an intellectual property advisor first. They can advise you on the best course of action to take.

Assignment of copyright notices

On a few very rare occasions I have employed an outsourcer (ghost-writer) to write specialist books for my publishing business. Before we agree a fee for the work I also state very clearly that they must sign an '**assignment of copyright notice**' once the work is completed. This notice is also sometimes referred to as a 'Transfer of copyright' agreement.

This assignment of copyright form basically assigns the rights of the written work to me once I have paid the agreed fee. This form then provides proof that I actually own the rights to the intellectual property they have written, and that they have no rights to the work at any time in the future. The reason why I ask a ghost-writer to sign the form is that I do not want them approaching me at any time during the future to ask for royalty payments.

The following is an example of an assignment of copyright notice for a book which you can use. Please ensure you take legal advice before using it:

ASSIGNMENT OF COPYRIGHT (EXAMPLE ONLY)

This Assignment of Copyright (the "Assignment") is made and entered on the DATE GOES HERE, by and between XXXXXX ("Author") and XXXXXX ("Assignee") (collectively referred to as the "Parties").

Whereas,

    i. The Author is the sole creator and owner of **NAME OF THE WRITTEN WORKS GOES HERE** and

    ii. The Author wishes to assign his/her copyright to Assignee.

Now, therefore, for valuable consideration, receipt and sufficiency of which are hereby acknowledged, the Parties agree as follows:

1. **ASSIGNMENT:** In consideration of **NAME OF THE WRITTEN WORKS GOES HERE** by Assignee to Author, Author hereby assigns, sells and transfers to Assignee all of his/her rights, title and interest in and to the Work, including, but not limited to: (i) all rights under copyright for the full legal term of copyright and all renewals, extensions, revisions and revivals together with all accrued rights of action throughout the world in any form and in any language (including all media, both now known or later developed) and any registrations and copyright applications relating thereto, and (ii) all income, royalties or claims relating to the Work due on or after the date of this Assignment.

2. **AUTHOR'S REPRESENTATIONS:** Author represents and warrants that he/she is the sole creator and owner of the Work, and has all rights, title and interest in and to the copyright in the Work and the power to enter into this Assignment. Author further represents and warrants that the rights transferred in this Assignment are free of lien, encumbrance or adverse claim.

3. **FURTHER ASSURANCES:** Author will co-operate fully to do all such further acts and things and execute or sign any further documents, instruments, notices or consents as may be reasonable and necessary or desirable to give full effect to the arrangements contemplated by this Agreement.

4. **BINDING EFFECT:** The covenants and conditions contained in this Assignment shall apply to and bind the Parties and their heirs, legal representatives, successors and permitted assigns.

5. **GOVERNING LAW:** This Assignment shall be governed by and construed in accordance with the laws of England and Wales. Any disputes arising from matters relating to this Agreement shall be exclusively subject to the jurisdiction of the courts of England and Wales.

IN WITNESS WHEREOF, the Parties have caused this Assignment to be executed on the day and year first above written.

AUTHOR:

XXXXXX

Date and sign

ASSIGNEE:

XXXXXXX

Date and sign

NOTE: You can obtain a copy of this notice and other important documents at my website, www.BookPublishingAcademy.co.uk.

The use of images on your book covers or website

When you have your first book cover or website created you will undoubtedly want to add some images to it. Whatever you do, make sure you obtain a licence to use your chosen images. Some people think they can go online, search for images in Google and then simply use them freely on a commercial basis – this is untrue. I am aware of some authors and entrepreneurs who have been fined for using images on their website without permission. Do not just take images from the Internet and use them on your website unless you are 100% sure they are free to use. My advice is to use a **royalty-free stock image** website and pay for the licence to use the image(s). The fees in order to use the images are relatively cheap!

The safest way to find 'royalty free' images with appropriate licences is to pay for their use on 'image stock' websites such as:

www.istockphoto.com

www.fotolia.com

www.shutterstock.com

www.bigstockimages.com

www.123RF.com

You should be able to find the images you need for your book cover or website at any of the above websites, but be sure to check the licences first to ensure they are suitable for commercial use.

If you need to find more specific images to use that are more niche, you might find them at the following website:

www.photographersdirect.com

Here's one final thing with regards to use of images on book covers and on websites. If you are using images on your website then you should opt for a maximum image size of 72dpi. If you use images which have a higher resolution that this it can slow the speed of your website down considerably! If you are using images for book covers however, then they will need to be a minimum of 300dpi to ensure quality during reproduction and print.

How to check ghost-written work is unique

I often get asked by authors how they can check whether or not a piece of ghost-written work they have paid for is actually unique and not simply copied or plagiarised from a 3rd party. Copyscape.com is a free plagiarism checker. The software lets you detect duplicate content and check if your articles are original:

www.CopyScape.com

CHAPTER 12
OUTSOURCERS

Get instant access to over 32 hours' worth of online training videos and support at:

www.BookPublishingAcademy.co.uk

USING OUTSOURCERS

In order for your book to achieve profitability quickly you will need to keep your production costs to an absolute minimum. Whether you are getting your book cover created, getting your manuscript converted to Kindle, or getting a website built to promote your book(s), you will naturally want to keep your costs down whilst maintaining quality.

The title of this book, 'How to write a book, get it published and keep all the profits', aims to teach you how to make your writing and publishing ventures profitable, and it is this particular chapter that will help you to do just that. One of the main reasons why I manage to generate 6-figure net profits year in, year out is because I am highly-effective at outsourcing.

"Successful outsourcing will not only allow you to focus on what you do best, writing the content, but it will also help you to find other ways to promote your book and expand your range of titles. By building relationships with your outsourcers that are based on trust and respect you will be able to create a publishing team that can accomplish just about anything…and give you much deserved time-off in the process."

The official definition of outsourcing is as follows:

'To obtain (goods or a service) from an outside supplier, in place of an internal source'

I personally prefer to define it as:

'To obtain (goods or a service) from an outside supplier to MASSIVELY increase the profits in your publishing business'

At the time of writing I employ just one member of part-time staff. Despite only physically employing one person, I have managed to compete with many of the larger independent publishers within the UK. Whenever I publish a book I will always aim to make it as profitable as possible, and I want you to do the same.

The pros and cons of outsourcing

- There is a massive pool of talent out there in the world today at your fingertips.

- You can outsource literally everything within your writing and publishing business!

- Outsourcers allow you to concentrate on what you are GOOD at.

- You don't have to speak to, or ever meet the outsourcers.

- Outsourcing can be very cost-effective, which means more money in your pocket.

- Outsourcing can triple or even quadruple your profits.

- The cost of living in many countries outside of the UK or US is far lower – therefore, the cost of outsourcing is a lot cheaper, too.

- There are some really good outsourcers for you to tap in to.

- Outsourcers can work whilst you are asleep due to the time difference.

- If an outsourcer cannot work due to sickness or holiday, they don't get paid.

- When you hire full or part-time staff within your business you are bound by employment and other laws within the UK. When you hire outsourcers you are only bound by the terms and conditions of the website from which you hire them from and your own contract (which you control) between yourself and the outsourcer.

There also a number of disadvantages to outsourcing too:

- There are so many outsourcers and outsourcing websites out there it is hard to determine who is genuine and who is not.

- It can be confusing, unless you know what you are doing.

- It is hard to let go and trust people with your work, especially if you are not going to meet the outsourcer or even speak to them.

- Outsourcers can potentially damage or even ruin your business.
- It can be difficult to communicate with them if their English is not very good.

Although the disadvantages do put many people off using outsourcers, my advice is to give it a try and see how you get on as it can be extremely advantageous. During the following sections I will teach you how to out-source for success.

What can I outsource?

With regards to writing and publishing books, you can outsource just about everything from writing the content for all or part of a book, through to type-setting and Kindle conversion. Here is a list of just some of the areas you can outsource within a publishing business:

- o Book writing
- o Book cover design.
- o Logo creation and branding.
- o Proofreading/editing.
- o Typesetting.
- o Printing.
- o Customer service/care.
- o eBook/Kindle conversion.
- o Website sales-copy.
- o Advertising/marketing and Public Relations (PR).
- o Website design/development.
- o Social media management.
- o Google and other search engine pay-per-click advertising.
- o Search engine optimisation.

Although I write my own books 99% of the time, I do sometimes come up with book ideas where I feel I do not have sufficient knowledge or expertise in the book subject area to do the content justice. As a result I will need to find a competent and proficient ghost-writer to create the content on my behalf.

Where to find outsourcers

There are many outsourcing companies available online for you to choose from. A comprehensive list is provided below:

- Odesk.com
- Elance.com
- Freelancer.com
- 99Designs.com
- AgentSolo.com
- AllFreelancedWork.com
- ContractedWork.com
- CoroFlot.com
- CraigsList.org
- DesignQuote.net
- GetACoder.com
- GetAFreelancer.com
- Guru.com
- Fiverr.com
- Freelancers.net
- FreelanceSwitch.com
- Freelance.com
- HireTheWorld.com
- iFreeLance.com
- Krop.com
- PeoplePerHour.com
- Proz.com
- ScriptLance.com
- SoloGig.com
- TranslatorsCafe.com
- RentACoder.com

Whilst there are many outsourcing websites to choose from, I actually only ever use a few in order to carry out all of my outsourcing requirements, namely ODesk.com, Elance.com, and Fiverr.com. Here is what I use each of these outsourcing websites for within my publishing business:

ODesk.com – Typesetting, book cover design, website design and website coding/development.

Elance.com – Proofreading, editing, article writing, and sometimes ghost-writing.

Fiverr.com – the creation of web-based videos to help promote my books and services.

Of course, the choice is yours with regards to which outsourcing website(s) you choose, but if you are looking for just one website that will offer you a place to outsource everything, then I recommend ODesk.com.

An alternative great place to get your book cover design created

www.99Designs.com is a great place to get your book cover designed. It is slightly different from a standard outsourcing website in the fact that lots of designers will create your book cover or logo for you based on your brief, and then you decide which one you like. The designer's book you choose will end up being the one who wins your money! Here's a more detailed explanation as to how it works:

STEP 1 - Build a design brief for the designers to work from

First of all you need to tell the designers what you want in your design. In order to do this you will need to answer the questions in 99designs.com's simple online brief.

STEP 2 - Choose a design package

The next step is to choose from one of four different design packages which are clearly explained on their website. Once you have chosen a package you pay up front, before 99designs.com then launches your contest in their marketplace. A higher price will mean a bigger designer prize for the chosen designer, which means you will get more designers competing for your prize!

STEP 3 - Receive dozens of designs

Once the contest is launched, designers then get to work before submitting their designs direct to your account. You can log in each day to view the new designs.

STEP 4 – Provide feedback to the designers

You will have the opportunity to give feedback to your designers so that you get the EXACT book cover design you want. You have the option to use ratings, comments and private messages to help designers shape their ideas to your needs. The more detailed your feedback, the easier it will be to get the design for your book you really want.

STEP 5 - Pick the winner

After 7 days has passed you need to pick the winner before signing the copy-right agreement. 99Designs.com will then transfer the prize money to the designer before you download your new design and use it however you like.

How to outsource successfully

The first step to outsourcing success is to decide what exactly you want to outsource within your publishing business. In order to achieve this I will write a list of things that I am not particular good at – this list will usually be the list of tasks I end up outsourcing. Here's what my list will look like:

List of tasks I need to outsource

- Book cover design
- Book typesetting
- eBook conversion
- Website design and sales copy
- Proofreading and editing
- Ghost-writing guides I have no expertise in or knowledge of

Once I have compiled my list I will then choose an outsourcing website in which to post my jobs. Let's assume I want to publish a book called 'How to climb Mount Everest', but I do not have any expertise or knowledge of the subject.

Once I have opened my ODesk.com account I will then post the following job:

TITLE – Competent and professional writer required for 'how to' guide.

I am seeking a highly competent and professional English author to write a 25,000 work book entitled 'How To Climb Mount Everest'. The book must consist of the following chapters:

- About Mount Everest
- Why do people climb it?
- The risks associated with climbing Mount Everest
- Mental state vs. physical state
- Preparing to climb
- Equipment you will need
- Financing your trip
- Base camp
- Advanced base camp
- Camp 1
- Camp 2
- Camp 3
- Camp 4 and Entering the Death-Zone
- Summit Day
- You're only half way there at the top!
- Useful links and resources

IMPORTANT NOTES:

1. The work must be unique, genuine and not copied from any websites or otherwise.

2. The content must be written in English as it is aimed predominantly at the UK market.

3. Upon completion of the project you will be required to sign a transfer of copyright agreement which transfers the copyright and intellectual property of the works over to me.

4. I require the completed written document to be supplied in Microsoft Word, font Arial and size 12, with 1.5 paragraph spacing.

5. The final deliverable written works must be delivered within 8 weeks.

6. The written works must be free from errors.

Whenever you upload a job to an outsourcing website make sure your job brief details exactly what you want, down to the minute detail. You will see in my job post that I have included 6 important notes. These enable me to have full control over the project, and they also ensure that I will not run into problems later down the line. When writing your job post you need to assume the outsourcer does not know anything about your job or what you want. Make sure you spoon-feed the outsourcers.

Now I will provide you with a sample outsourcing job post for a book cover designer:

TITLE – Competent and professional designer required to create book cover.

I am seeking an experienced, professional and competent designer to create a book cover for me based on the following details:

- The book size will be 242mm x 170mm x 12mm spine.
- I require the designer to supply all royalty free commercial use images for the cover as part of the cost.
- I require a hi-resolution 300dpi front book image cover and a full hi-resolution jacket cover (print-ready) as part of the price.
- You will be required to add a barcode and ISBN number to the artwork, which will be supplied by me.
- You will be required to sign a transfer of copyright agreement upon completion of the design which hands over full copyright of the works to me.
- The title and description for the book cover will be supplied once the successful candidate is selected.

You will note that I have not provided specific details of what the book subject is about at this stage. The reason for this is because I do not want anyone on the outsourcing website to see or steal my book idea. Once I have chosen the book cover designer I will then provide that particular individual with a full brief relating to the title of the book cover.

You will notice that I did not hold back the book title and chapters within the ghost-writer job post. This was simply because I am looking for a particular specialist ghost-writer who is capable of writing this type of content, and therefore I need to be specific from the outset.

My top tips for successful outsourcing

TIP #1 - DO NOT choose an outsourcer solely on price

"Some of the best outsourcers cost only slightly more than the cheapest..."

This is your business/future, so choose your outsourcers very carefully. People tend to jump in with both feet and take the first/cheapest person who comes along. This is often a mistake. Take the time to look at the outsourcer's credentials, experience, reviews, and previous work.

TIP #2 - Develop and use systems

"Without the use of outsourcing systems, you will fail."

Your system must include:

- A system for getting the BEST outsourcers.
- What you want your outsourcers to do for you and by when!
- How you want the work to be done.
- An agreed price/payment system.
- Agreed terms and conditions.

Remember to spoon-feed the outsourcers – don't just assume they know what you want them to create for you.

TIP #3 - Use <u>ONLY</u> the best outsourcers

"Outsourcing is BIG business now and lots of people are bidding for your cash – choose your outsourcers very carefully."

Ways to get the best outsourcers:

- Use the most popular outsourcing websites, but do take care. (ODesk. com, Elance.com and Fiverr.com)
- Check feedback and references of all outsourcers you are considering hiring.
- Be on the lookout for recommendations. Some of my most cherished outsourcers have come from recommendations.
- Consider getting a mentor and use their outsourcers. My website www.BookPublishingAcademy.co.uk will provide you with a list of the outsourcers I have used over the years.

TIP #4 - Pay your outsourcers fast!

"I usually get a faster/better service because I always pay on time."

The aim is to build a strong working relationship with your outsourcers that will last for many years. By paying them promptly you will get a better and faster service. Believe it or not, I only use a handful of outsourcers at any one time.

TIP #5 - Test your outsourcers before you agree to use them

"There are so many outsourcers out there who are all competing for your business that it can be hard to determine who is the best and has your best interests at heart."

Ways to test your outsourcers:

- Request an 'action-point' in the job description for those who apply. For example, I sometimes ask people to contact me using a reference number such as 'JOB2014'. Those people who contact me without making reference to the number have clearly not read my brief and will therefore not get hired!

- Consider trying out an outsourcer on a DIFFERENT task to the one you really want them to do (max. 1 hour).

- Keep tight control over the outsourcers 'hours' in the early stages until you can trust them 100%.

TIP #6 - For larger, more complex jobs, consider using video to explain your brief

"The more money you are spending, consider creating a short video tutorial to explain exactly what you want the outsourcer to do."

- Using a video tutorial for more complex job requests will ensure that no stone gets left unturned.

- You can use a tool such as Camtasia Techsmith (www.techsmith.com) to record a simple PowerPoint presentation.

- One of the most important elements of subcontracting is making sure you and the subcontractor are on the same page and that there are no surprises.

TIP #7 - Negotiate support for after the job is complete

"Once the job is complete and you have made your payment you need to have the opportunity to go back to the outsourcer if required – a good outsourcer will not have a problem with this."

- Negotiate on-going support after the work is completed. I usually ask for 7 days support after a designer has created a book cover design or formatted/typeset my manuscript. This enables me to go back for minor changes if needed, and it also ensures the outsourcer gets paid promptly, too.

- This is especially important for web development based projects.

- Agree a time-frame for the outsourcer to respond to all support requests.

TIP #8 - Don't pay for the job up-front unless using escrow

"Paying for a job in full up-front gives you no protection. The outsourcer may not stick to the agreed time-frame if you have already paid them for the job in advance."

- Negotiate an up-front fee to be paid in advance – usually 50%.

- If you use an outsourcing website or platform you will need to pay the money into a holding account – this may sometimes be via escrow.

- Only release the money when you are 100% happy with the work, unless you have negotiated ongoing support.

TIP #9 - Clarify the ownership of the work when negotiating the deal

"It is very important that you negotiate the ownership of the work in advance. You want to have ownership to the copyright of the works, especially when outsourcing writing of books and articles etc."

- You can get caught out months or even years down the line if you do not verify the ownership of the intellectual property.

- Make sure you own the copyright or intellectual property relating to the works before agreeing a contract.

- A simple email confirming that you own the IP may suffice: "Can you please confirm that I will own the copyright/intellectual property to all elements of the work once completed and full payment has been made?"

- Insist on a Transfer of Copyright Agreement for books which are ghost-written.

TIP #10 - Leave positive feedback where credit is due

"I take great pride in the fact that I have excellent relationships with ALL my outsourcers. Very rarely do I receive work which is not to an outstanding standard."

- Remember to think about the future. You are looking to have a small team of outsourcers who you can go back to time and time again.

- Many people forget to give credit when it is due. If the work is good, say so.

- I have a small number of outstanding outsourcers that do all of my work. I get priority treatment from my outsourcers.

- Here's what I might write in the feedback section of my outsourcer if the work has been good: "As usual, the work was carried out to a very high standard. XXXX is great to work with and always on-time. I would recommend her to anyone."

To help you learn more about the process of outsourcing I have created over 32 hours' worth of online training videos. You can gain access to these at the following website: www.BookPublishingAcademy.co.uk.

CHAPTER 13
REGISTERING YOUR BUSINESS

Get instant access to over 32 hours' worth of online training videos and support at:

www.BookPublishingAcademy.co.uk

REGISTERING YOUR BUSINESS

In this chapter of the guide I will provide advice and tips for setting up your publishing business. Whilst I appreciate this information may not be relevant to everybody who reads this book, I feel it is important to cover this subject in order to ensure your business gets off to the right start. Please note: before you decide which company set up is best for you and your needs, please consult a qualified accountant.

THE DIFFERENT TYPES OF COMPANY AND HOW TO REGISTER

SOLE TRADER

Sole trading (on your own) is the simplest way to run a business. Many authors who write and self-publish their books will choose this simple set-up.

One of the major benefits is that you do not have to pay any registration fees and you get to keep all of the profits. However, you will have to keep all of your own records and accounts, which will mean you'll need to employ a bookkeeper and an accountant unless you carry out these functions yourself. When I first started my book publishing business I did everything myself. I soon realised that having a great bookkeeper and accountant takes a lot of the pressure away from you. This will also enable you to concentrate on what you are probably really good at – writing books!

The only real downside to a sole trader business is that you are personally liable for any debts that your business runs up. This can make sole trading a risky option for businesses that need a lot of investment.

Setting up and registering a sole trader business is relatively simple. All you need to do in order to register as a sole trader is to download and complete form CWF1 from the HM Revenue & Customs:

www.hmrc.gov.uk/

PARTNERSHIPS

In a partnership there are always two or more people who share the risks, costs and responsibilities of the business. The benefit of partnerships is that they are a simple way for two or more people to own and run a business together. Partners are personally responsible for any debts that the business incurs, and they are all self-employed.

The difference between a partnership and a limited company is that the partnership has no legal existence apart from the partners themselves. If one of the partners resigns, dies, or unfortunately goes bankrupt, then the partnership will have to be dissolved. This type of set up might be most suited to two people (perhaps partners) who want to set up a book writing and publishing business together.

Setting up and registering a partnership

There are 3 different types of partnership, and they are detailed as follows:

General partners

In this type of partnership general partners invest in the business. They also take a share of the profits and are involved in the day-to-day running of the business. The risk with a partnership of this nature is that each partner is fully liable for any debts that the partnership may have. Therefore, each partner could lose all that they have invested and still be liable for more than their initial investment if the partnership gets into trouble. Every partnership must have at least one general partner.

Sleeping or dormant partners

Sleeping partners invest money in the business and share in its profits. However, they do not take part in the day-to-day running of the business. Like general partners, they are still fully liable for the partnership's debts.

Companies

It is possible for a company to be an officer of a partnership. If this happens then the company has the same rights and responsibilities within the partnership as the other partners. Partnerships whose officers are all companies have to prepare "partnership accounts" and send these to Companies House or the Northern Ireland Companies Registry every year. The officers of these partnerships must also attach a copy of these accounts to their own company accounts when they submit these to Companies House.

LIMITED LIABILITY PARTNERSHIP (LLP)

A limited liability partnership (LLP) is similar to an ordinary partnership, in that a number of individuals or limited companies share in the risks, costs, responsibilities and profits of the business.

The difference here is that the liability is limited to the amount of money the LLP invested in the business and to any personal guarantees they have given to raise finance. This means that members have limited protection if the business runs into trouble.

Setting up a Limited Liability Partnership (LLP)

A limited liability partnership (LLP) agreement is very similar to a normal partnership agreement. The added benefit of an LLP is that it offers a reduced personal responsibility for business debts. This is something that is worth taking into consideration when starting your business.

Unlike sole traders and partners of ordinary partnerships, the limited liability partnership itself is responsible for the debts that it incurs. However, this does not apply if individual members have personally guaranteed a loan to the business.

Limited liability partnerships have to meet similar requirements to limited companies, and therefore they are not easy to run. The main purpose of an LLP business structure is to be used for profit-making businesses. It is advised that non-profit making businesses should not use this type of business structure.

To register an LLP, please visit the Companies House website at: www.companieshouse.gov.uk

You should never underestimate the importance of a quality accountant and bookkeeper. A good bookkeeper and accountant can save you the cost of their monthly or annual fee, so choose them carefully. The following accountant comes highly recommended:

www.a4g-llp.co.uk

LIMITED COMPANY

Limited companies exist in their own right and are registered through Companies House. This means that the company's finances are distinct from the personal finances of their owners. Shareholders may be individuals or other companies. They are not responsible for the company's debts (unless they have personally guaranteed a bank loan, for example). However, they may lose the money they originally invested in the company if it fails.

Setting up and registering a limited company (private or public)

Basically there are two different types of limited company. These are as follows:

- Private Limited Company
- Public Limited Company

Many small businesses that start out choose to become a private limited company. For example, when I started my own publishing business I set it up as a Limited company, and it still exists in this format today. The main differences between a private limited company and a public limited company are as follows:

- Public limited companies can raise money by selling shares on the stock market, whereas private limited companies are not permitted to do this.
- Public limited companies must have share capital of at least £50,000.
- Public limited companies must have two shareholders, two directors and a qualified company secretary.

At any point a private limited company that is limited by shares can convert into a public limited company, but it must re-register with Companies House in order to do so.

Limited by shares or by guarantee?

Private limited companies are limited by shares, and they are owned by their shareholders. The benefit of this ruling is that the shareholders who paid in full for their shares are not liable for the company's debts. However, any shareholders who have part-paid for their shares (if applicable) are liable for the outstanding amount owing to the company for their shares. It is also possible to set up a private limited company that is limited by guarantee. In this type of company, the people who form it agree on liability limits when it is established. This structure is often used by social enterprises to limit the personal liability of their directors and trustees.

To register or set up a private or public limited company, please visit the Companies House website at:

www.companieshouse.gov.uk

Once you have applied to set up your company you will receive notification as to whether your application has been successful or not.

In addition to registering your private business as a company, you must also:

- Display the company name clearly on the outside of all offices or other places of business.

- Display the company name clearly on all your business stationery, including letters, invoices, receipts and cheques.

- Detail your company's place of registration, registered number and registered office address on all business letters and order forms.

- Send all the necessary registration documents and forms, fully completed and signed, to the Registrar of Companies.

- Contact HM Revenue & Customs for advice to ensure that you are acting within your legal responsibilities.

Registration documents and forms required to set up your Limited company

In order to set up as a limited company within the UK, you must send several documents and completed forms to Companies House. If you are setting up your company in Northern Ireland you will need to register with the Companies Registry for Northern Ireland. Here is a list of the documentation you will have to complete and register:

- A Memorandum of Association, giving details of the company's name, location and what it will do.

- Articles of Association, describing how the company will be run, the rights of the shareholders and the powers of the company's directors.

- Form 10 (Statement of the First Directors, Secretary and Registered Office), giving details of the company's registered office and the names and addresses of its directors and company secretary. The equivalent of this form in Northern Ireland is Form 21.

- Form 12 (Declaration of Compliance with the Requirements of the Companies Act), stating that the company meets all the legal requirements of incorporation. The equivalent form in Northern Ireland is Form 23.

If you are intending on setting out as a self-publisher who publishes just a small number of books then it may be wise to set up as a sole trader. However, if you have bigger aspirations then you may decide to set up a Limited Company. Be sure to take advice from a qualified accountant first. Let's now move on and take a look at the financial management and organisation of your book writing and publishing business.

CHAPTER 14

FINANCIAL MANAGEMENT AND ORGANISATION

Get instant access to over 32 hours' worth of online training videos and support at:

www.BookPublishingAcademy.co.uk

FINANCIAL MANAGEMENT AND ORGANISATION

When you start your new book writing and publishing business, time will need to be spent on financial organisation. Having the book ideas and the drive and determination to succeed are paramount to your success. However, poor financial management and planning will adversely affect your levels or profitability and future sustainability within the industry.

The way in which you handle your finances will be critical to the success of your writing and publishing business. If you fail to keep on top of your bookkeeping or your bookkeeping is disorganised then the viability and success of your business venture will be compromised. Conversely, keeping bookwork up to date will help you through the lean times and allow your business to grow.

What to do first

I recommend that before you start trading you get in contact with the local offices of the Inland Revenue and HM Revenue and Customs. Either call them or make an appointment to see them. You can find a number of useful helplines on the Government's advisory website using the following contact numbers:

Business Link Helpline

0845 600 9006

Monday to Friday, 9am to 6pm

Business Wales Helpline

0300 060 3000

Monday to Friday, 8am to 6pm

Business Gateway (Scotland)

0845 609 6611

Monday to Friday, 8am to 6pm

Invest Northern Ireland

0800 181 4422

Monday to Friday, 8am to 5pm

When you make contact with the relevant section explain the details of your business plan and ask them what you need to do. They'll provide you with advice, leaflets, and a selection of forms such as VAT registration that you may need to complete before you begin trading. This is important. If you start off with all the necessary information it will make the bookkeeping process much easier. It also helps to have a contact within the local offices that you can call whenever you run into any difficulties.

As I mentioned earlier, if you are simply planning on writing and publishing just one book then you may not need to go through the above process. However, if you have big plans, like I did, then you should start as you mean to go on.

Business Bank Account

You will need a business bank account if you are running a business. You simply cannot survive without one. It is the focal point of your business finances, showing all the financial transactions of your business. A business bank account is where you pay money in, pay suppliers and your work-force, draw out petty cash, and complete all of the other essential financial transactions involved in running a business. It is also the place that your royalties will get paid into.

If you're a sole trader, this will keep your business account separate from your personal finances. Having a business bank account is also essential to calculating tax. A business bank account can in some cases give you access to support, advice and finance. You will need to decide which bank to use. Before you start comparing different banks it's worth knowing the products and services they may offer.

Bank facilities for business owners

- **Deposits**: Paying in cash and cheques and accepting your Amazon royalties.

- **Withdrawals**: Taking out cash through an ATM or at a branch.

- **Payment by cheque**: Use of a business chequebook, which can sometimes be personalised with your company logo.

- **Automatic money transfers**: Direct debits and direct credits. These facilities will be required so that you can pay for necessities such as printed books and paying your outsourcers on time.

- **Night safe**: For depositing money when the bank is closed.

- **Balance enquiry and statements**: For keeping track of your finances.

- **Company debit card**: This will debit an amount immediately from your business account. In most cases the transactions are free and there is no annual fee.

- **Company credit card**: A charge card (such as Barclaycard or MasterCard) that can be issued to key members of staff. Repayments are made monthly from your business current account (usually interest free credit). There is usually a fee per transaction, an annual fee or both.

- **Overdraft and loan facilities**: Short-term financing, subject to an application procedure.

- **Asset finance**: Leasing and hire purchase facilities to enable you to buy equipment.

- **Factoring and invoice discounting**: Short-term borrowing against the value of unpaid invoices.

- **Commercial mortgage**: Funding to help you buy a business property. Often up to 80% of the purchase can be financed by the bank.

- **Deposit accounts**: A lot of banks have business deposit accounts with higher interest than a current account for any reserve funds your business may have.

- **Merchant services**: If you want to accept credit and debit card payments from customers, you will need a merchant account. This is provided by a bank, but to get one you will often need two years' trading history and audited accounts. Once set-up you will be charged an annual fee plus a percentage of every transaction.

- **Insurance**: The larger banks will often offer their customers insurance cover for business interruption, health, loan repayments and more.

- **Support**: Most of the larger banks offer resources and support to help you run your business. For example, you may be assigned a relationship manager who will offer business advice. The bank may also provide seminars, educational literature or bookkeeping software.

- **Introductory offers**: The main banks offer special introductory offers to start-ups. This is usually a period of free banking for 12-24 months.

VALE ADDED TAX (VAT)

If you're in business, you must register for VAT if your VAT taxable turnover for the previous twelve months is more than £79,000. This figure is known as the VAT registration threshold. The threshold changes - usually once a year announced in the Budget - so you should regularly check your turnover against the current threshold.

You must also register for VAT if either of the following applies:

- you think your VAT taxable turnover may go over the threshold in the next 30 days alone
- you take over a VAT-registered business as a going concern

VAT quarterly returns must be completed and sent to HM Customs and Excise, along with any payment due. The VAT forms are very simple - just a single page, in fact - and usually work in the company's favour. This is because although you must pay VAT on any income generated, you can claim back VAT paid on some goods and services, such as office supplies, vehicle servicing, fuel and so on. So the extra accounting is definitely worth it, and even companies whose turnover is less than the VAT limit can still register voluntarily. Not all products and services attract the standard VAT rate, so it's worth contacting your local HMC&E office to request one of their introductory videos, which will explain the basics of VAT accounting.

Keep yourself up to date with the latest VAT information and rates by listening to the Budget. This will be done by your accountant/bookkeeper, but it is good for you and your business to be aware of this information. Remember you are expected to account for every business-related penny spent and you are expected to show each month's profit/loss and income/expenditure in sufficient detail so that the tax can be clearly calculated.

Please note: physical 'printed' books are not currently eligible for VAT, whereas Kindle books and eBooks are. This has confused many people within the book publishing industry, but unfortunately it is a fact that we all have to deal with. So, if you want to sell both a printed book and an eBook version on your website, you will have to add VAT (currently 20%) to the sale price of the eBook only, and not the printed book.

Accountancy software

Buying an accountancy software package can slash the amount of time and effort you put into managing your finances. In the early stages you could use the services of a freelance bookkeeper or your accountant, as mentioned earlier, who will have the software and keep your books up to date on a monthly basis for a fee.

The top 10 financial management tips and advice:

Financial Management Tip 1

Talk to the local offices of the Inland Revenue and HM Revenue and Customs if you are considering setting up your own book publishing business. Either call them or book an appointment. If possible, do this before you start to trade, as this will save complications at a later date. As mentioned previously, start as you mean to go on!

Financial Management Tip 2

Get yourself a business bank account. Look around at what's on offer, and use all the facilities the bank has to offer you - you can never get too much advice. You should also look for a period of free business banking. This essentially means you will not get charged any business transaction fees for a set period of time once you open your account.

Financial Management Tip 3

Right from the start, keep records of payments and sales etc. Keep all your receipts as, again, failing to do this can cause problems for your business accounts in the future.

Financial Management Tip 4

Get yourself an accountant and book an appointment to see them. They will give you advice and information on all your business accounting matters.

Financial Management Tip 5

Get yourself a freelance bookkeeper to keep your accounts in order on a monthly basis. This will save you the time you would spend doing it yourself and free you up to drive your business forward. A bookkeeper who I fully recommend can be found here:

www.breakspearnorris.co.uk/

Financial Management Tip 6

Keep up-to-date with financial business matters, from VAT to corporation tax. Although your accountant will know all this information, it is beneficial for you to know it too so that you can plan and budget your finances in order to develop your business.

Financial Management Tip 7

Know your business. Know how much profit percentage you make and know your turnover. Again, this will enable you to move your business forward or budget where needed.

Financial Management Tip 8

Keep paperwork and receipts for everything. Keep all paperwork to do with the financial side of your business, even if you think it is not relevant. It is better to have some irrelevant paperwork than to be missing the records your accountant or bookkeeper will be chasing you for. With regards to receipts, your bookkeeper and accountant will be able to advise what you can and cannot claim for.

Financial Management Tip 9

Make sure you put by money each month to cover any future VAT bill (if registered) or corporation tax bill. This will prevent you from receiving that large tax bill that has not been accounted for.

Financial Management Tip 10

Although the financial side of your book writing and publishing business is extremely important, do not spend hours and hours on it (use your bookkeeper/accountant). The important element of your business is your entrepreneurial skills, and your ability to write great content for your books.

Profit & loss accounts and reading a balance sheet

By law, companies in the UK are required to produce financial statements each year. These statements appear in Company Reports. There are two main financial statements:

1. The profit and loss account, and

2. The balance sheet.

Once again, this information may not be relevant to some authors just starting out; however, I feel it is important to get to know all aspects of a business if it is to be successful.

The profit and loss (P&L) account

This account can be updated regularly, and it shows how much profit or loss your business is making.

The top section of a P&L account is known as the trading account for a business that buys and sells items, e.g. a bookshop. What is known as the gross profit is calculated by deducting cost of sales from turnover.

For example:

The profit and loss account for a bookshop

	£
Turnover	200,000
Cost of sales	120,000
Gross profit	80,000

Turnover is sometimes referred to as **sales revenue,** and it is calculated by multiplying the number of items sold by their average price.

For example, if the average price of a book is £10.

The number of books sold is 10,000.

The turnover is therefore: 10,000 x £10 = £100,000

Cost of sales is the cost of buying in the items in order to trade them, in this case the cost of buying the books. For example, the bookshop may buy in books at an average cost of £5 each. Let's assume that it has bought in 10,000 books.

Cost of sales is therefore: 10,000 x £5 = £50,000

Gross profit is calculated by deducting cost of sales from turnover.

Gross profit is therefore: £100,000 - £50,000 = £50,000

We now need to examine the next part of the P&L account.

As well as the cost of sales, a business will incur overhead costs. These costs can not directly be related to each unit of output made or sold - hence the name overheads.

Overheads are typically referred to as expenses in the P&L account.

Typical expenses for a business include items such as heating and lighting costs, insurance, and advertising. General administrative costs of running a business appear as administrative expenses.

The net profit of a business is calculated by deducting the expenses from the gross profit figure.

Turnover - Cost of Sales = Gross Profit

Gross Profit - Expenses = Net Profit

The Balance Sheet

The Balance Sheet is like a snapshot taken at a particular moment in time giving a summary of the overall financial position of a business. Businesses need to use assets in order to generate wealth. Assets are the things that a business owns, or sums that are owed to the business at any one moment in time.

The business obtains the finance for these assets from two main sources:

1. **Internally** (inside the business) from capital raised from the business owners (the shareholders in the case of a company).

2. **Externally** - for example, in the form of loans, and other forms of finance; this will need to be repaid.

When you set up a business, the business becomes a legal body in its own right.

• Internal finance (shareholders' funds) is owed to shareholders.

• External finance is owed to people outside the business - liabilities.

The Balance Sheet will therefore balance because;

In simple terms this shows that the value of a business's assets is financed by the two groups - 1.Internal (owner's capital), 2.External (liabilities).

A balance sheet typically appears in a vertical format.

The balance sheet starts off by listing all the assets. Next come the liabilities, and finally the owners' capital is shown - to 'balance' the balance sheet.

This is what a typical Balance Sheet looks like

	£000	£000
Fixed Assets		2000
Current Assets		
Stock	500	
Debitors	1000	
Cash	500	
	2000	
Creditors due within one year	1000	
Net current assets		1000
Creditors due after more than one year	2000	
Total net assets	1000	
Shareholder's Funds	1000	

What does the balance sheet show?

1. The fixed assets show assets that will be kept in the business to generate wealth for the company over a period of time, e.g. machines, computers and buildings.

2. In contrast, current assets are turned into cash in the short term. For example, a trading company will buy stock, which it then sells on credit. When the debtors pay up, they will pay in cash. This cash can then be used to buy more stock.

3. Creditors due within one year shows the short term liabilities of the business, i.e. money that the company must pay within the next twelve months.

4. Net current assets show the current assets minus the current liabilities. It is important to have enough current assets (money coming in in the short term) to pay short term creditors (called short term liabilities). In the example shown the current assets are £2,000, and the current liabilities are £1,000.

Therefore net current assets = £1,000.

5. Creditors due after more than one year are the longer term liabilities of the business, for example long term bank loans and mortgage repayments.

6. The total net assets of the business are calculated by taking away all the liabilities (short and long term) from all of the assets (short and long term).

Total net assets = (Fixed assets Current assets) - (Current liabilities Long-term liabilities).

7. Finally, the Balance Sheet is balanced. The Total Net Assets figure is £1000

(i.e. assets are greater than liabilities by £1000). The assets that are not financed by external liabilities are financed by the owners - therefore the owners' capital is £1000.

Business plans

No guide on how to write and publish your own books would be complete without the all-important business plan. A business plan will help you map out your book and publishing ideas, assess their viability, and form the basis and action plan for your new business in its early days.

The best business plans aren't long and complex: they explain only the most important information –what you want to achieve, how you will get there, and the things you need to do along the way.

The following business plan template has a suggested structure for the business plan. The contents and notes are what would be expected in a plan. However, they should be altered to suit your own requirements.

Before completing the document you will need to have done some research into competitor activity, pricing, the market for your services/products, etc.

Book Writing & Publishing Business Plan Template

(Insert the name of your book writing and publishing business here)

Date the business plan was last updated (month and year)

SECTION 1 - MANAGEMENT SUMMARY

This is a summary of the plan and is better left to last.

SECTION 2 - BACKGROUND OF THE BUSINESS OWNER(S)

Give a short personal and business background, showing areas that are relevant to your proposed business, including skills and experience that will be used in the business.

Include things that you need to learn to ensure you can run your business well. How will you learn the new skills? When do you plan to learn them?

- Why do you want to run your own book writing and publishing business?
- List any previous work experiences with regards to book writing & publishing.
- Qualifications and education within your chosen field.
- What knowledge/experience do you have of the book writing and publishing industry, and what training (if any) have you completed?
- Details of any future training courses you want to attend and complete – for example: www.BookPublishingCourses.com.
- Consider a SWOT (strengths, weaknesses, opportunities, threats) analysis
- Any additional information.

SECTION 3 - PRODUCT OR SERVICE OFFERED

- Give a detailed description of your book ideas, publishing aims and website.
- Use Bullet Points.
- Include pictures of proposed book cover ideas, logo or branding if relevant.

SECTION 4 - YOUR CUSTOMER/TARGET MARKET

Who are your target customers? How many are there? Why should anyone want to buy what you provide? What is your evidence for this and what market research has been carried out? Are there enough customers for your book writing and publishing business to be viable?

- Describe your typical customer in detail.
- Where are your customers based? (Amazon, Gardners books, Waterstones, own website etc.)
- What book category are you aiming to sell under? (Fiction, self-help, motivational etc.)
- What prompts or motivates your customers to buy your product/service?

Market Research

Provide evidence and detailed findings of your market research. Give facts rather than "your interpretation" of your proposed market. Be objective. You could use any of the following to help with your research:

- Questionnaires of any market research you have conducted to assess demand for your book(s) – provide a copy of any used.
- Details of your Google Keyword-Planner research.
- Word-of-mouth requests. For example, when I started the 'how2become' series of books many people were asking me for a book on how to become a train driver.

  - Is there a demand for your book?
  - How big is the market/demand? (use the Google Keyword Planner tool to assess the market)
  - Current trends up or down – again, use the Google Keyword Planner tool to asses seasonal trends. If you are writing fiction books then there will be increased demand in the build-up to Christmas, and also during holiday/term time.
  - Any important facts, statistics or even whether the market is seasonal or dependent on other external factors such as the New Year. For

example, demand for career, motivational and self-help books doubles during the early New Year.

- Your own knowledge or past work experience of your chosen niche.

If you are interested in or want to research statistics, good places to find information are:

www.upmystreet.com

www.businesslink.gov.uk

www.statistics.gov.uk

www.direct.gov

- What factors may help your customers to choose which authors or publishers to buy from? For example, will your niche book category sell better on Amazon or via the prominent High Street stores?

- Have you sold your book(s) to customers already?

SECTION 5 - COMPETITION

Who are your competitors, and how many are there?

- Direct Competitors – those selling similar books in your niche or category, i.e. if you are writing a book on how to write business plans, who are your competitors?

- Indirect Competitors – those selling alternative books that are similar, i.e. authors and publishers selling books in your category area but with different subjects and titles.

Once you have identified your competitors, write down how you will be different.

- Why should anyone want to buy from you and not from your competitors?

- What is you USP (Unique Selling Point) – Why are you different? Perhaps you offer FREE access to online training videos or a DVD with your book. These will offer 'added value' and can help to increase conversions. Perhaps you are the authority or expert in your chosen book area, whereas your competitors are not.

- What will your customers look for when buying from you? For example, do you have a unique brand or logo?

SECTION 6 - MARKETING AND PROMOTION

- What information/facts are you going to tell potential customers about your product/service to encourage them to buy from you? Think about your book description or website sales copy.

- What are the key main features or selling points of your book(s)?

- What is the benefit of your particular book(s) to your readers?

- What methods are you going to use to reach your potential customers? For example, will you match the book title to what people are searching for having used the Google Keyword Planner Tool?

- Why did you select these methods, and how will you measure the success or failure of your marketing?

- What offers and promotions are you going to use under each category below:-

- Attracting new customers? For example, within the content of your book will you draw people back to your website in order to capture their name and email address to help with future promotions?

- Building loyalty/retaining customers?

- Encouraging each customer to spend more? Consider the upsell process within your book, and also what other products or services you might be able to offer.

SECTION 7 - PRICING AND COSTING

- How have you arrived at your selling price? Look at the price point of your competitors. Do not automatically drop your prices to compete with them.

- What is the cost to you of producing this book?

- How much are your competitors charging?

SECTION 8 - SALES FORECAST

- What value of sales do you expect to make each month in the first year? Think carefully about how much you need to make to break even and also to live comfortably. Be honest with your figures.

- It is unlikely that your sales will be the same in every month of the year, so show your monthly sales estimates. These figures might be based on seasonal expectations for sales of your book.

- Show how you have calculated these and explain (in words) how you have arrived at the monthly values. For example, have you considered seasonality and other reasons why customers might spend more or less money with you in different months? Because I always sell more books in January of each year, I will always plan to publish more books in the months after this month because I will have more disposable income to invest on development.

- Give a summary of how confident you are of achieving the forecasted sales.

SECTION 9 - ADMIN & LEGAL REQUIREMENTS

- What paperwork do you need to put in place before you start trading: disclaimers within your book, terms and conditions of your website (if you have one), enquiry forms on your website so people can contact you, quote forms from trade customers, invoices, receipts etc? TIP: I use a fantastic little website to keep track of my invoices here: www.freshbooks.com.

- How are you going to keep control of all your business information, on a computer or manually? TIP: I recommend you save your intellectual property to your computer hard drive, but also back it up regularly to an external computer hard drive, too. The one I use is called 'ELEMENTS' and can be found on Amazon by searching for 'elements hard drive'. You can also find external hard drives at places such as PC World or Curry's.

- How will you keep your financial records? Consider a bookkeeper.

What legal aspects do you need to consider? Examples are:

- o Supply of Goods & Services Act.
- o Health & Safety (if people are visiting your office or place of work).
- o Copyright/patents etc.
- o Distance Selling Regulations.
- o Data Protection.

What types of insurance do you require? Examples are:

- o Public Liability.
- o Professional Indemnity.
- o Employers Liability.
- o Life Cover.
- o Stock/business asset cover.

SECTION 10 - START-UP COSTS

- List all costs incurred at start-up, including equipment already purchased for use in the business, and explain how you will fund this.
- Also include how much money you may be planning to borrow.

ITEM	DETAILS	COST (£)
Premises:		
Equipment:		
Transport:		
Materials/Stock:		
Utilities/Payments up front:		
Marketing:		
Other:		
TOTAL COSTS		£
Less Funds Injected/ items already paid for		£
LOAN Required		£

SECTION 11 - PERSONAL SURVIVAL BUDGET

Section		Monthly cost (£)
A Costs	Mortgage/rent	
	Council tax	
	Gas, electricity and oil	
	Water rates	
	All personal and property insurance	
	Clothing	
	Food and housekeeping	
	Telephone	
	Hire charges (TV, DVD etc.)	
	Subscriptions (clubs, magazines etc.)	
	Entertainment (meals and drinks)	
	Car tax, insurance, service and maintenance	
	Presents (Christmas/ birthdays etc)	
	Children's expenditure and presents	
	Credit card, loan and other personal debt	
	Holidays, outings etc	
	National Insurance	
	Other	
B	Total costs (£)	
C Income	Income from family/partner	
	Part time job	
	Working tax credit	
	Child benefits	
	Other benefits	
	Other	
D	Total income (£)	
E (B less D)	Total survival income required (£)	

Bookkeeping

Engaging a qualified bookkeeper is not about how much you pay, but about how much you save. Many authors, publishers and business owners in general underestimate the value of a talented bookkeeper, instead opting to have a bash at it themselves, but without the knowledge or interest your records will likely be poorly kept, tax overpaid, and allowances not claimed.

A qualified bookkeeper will provide you with financial reports regularly throughout the year, such as a Profit & Loss and Balance Sheet, providing month-on-month comparisons about your company's performance. These reports are key to the early identification of trends and changes in your financial position as an author and publisher.

Your bookkeeper will keep you compliant with HMRC, ensuring returns such as VAT, etc. are accurate and submitted on time, reducing your chance of being selected for an inspection by HMRC or receiving one of the many fines HMRC now has in place for poorly kept records, or returns submitted late or calculated inaccurately. Your bookkeeper will liaise between HMRC and you and between your Accountant and you, interpreting their jargon and ensuring your time is spent more valuably in making money by writing and self-publishing high quality books.

Your bookkeeper is also an excellent source of information for other business issues such as employing staff, a shoulder to cry on when times are hard, and someone to bounce ideas off.

Andrea at **www.breakspearnorris.co.uk** is highly recommended.

CHAPTER 15

USING THE INTERNET IN YOUR BOOK PUBLISHING BUSINESS

Get instant access to over 32 hours' worth of online training videos and support at:

www.BookPublishingAcademy.co.uk

USING THE INTERNET IN YOUR BOOK PUBLISHING BUSINESS

I feel it is important to dedicate a chapter to the internet and how it can help you to promote your book(s) and grow your publishing business in general. The vast majority of books I sell are now online, which is a great thing simply because it means I have fewer overheads and therefore my profits are higher. As more and more people switch to the internet to buy their books and general products/services, it is important that you have, at the very least, a basic understanding of how it works and how it can be used to promote and sell your book(s).

There are many different ways of using the Internet to your advantage as an author and self-publisher. It is a highly cost-effective business tool if used correctly and is a great way of reaching thousands of potential customers at just a click of a button. As already mentioned, Amazon receives over 80,000,000 per month, and this figure is set to rise in the coming years.

If you can create a book or a series of books that are universally in demand and accessible through the Internet then you are on to a winner. Here are just a few ideas of how the Internet can be used to a commercial advantage:

- With the Internet you are able to obtain up-to-date quality sales opportunities not readily available elsewhere. For example, we have already established that the Google Keyword Planner Tool is one invaluable resource in your armoury as an author and publisher that will tell you what type of information people are searching for online.

- Those authors and self-publishers who mail out to a list of subscribers or previous customers can gain financially. With post or even fax you pay for each separate mailing or call. With electronic mail the cost of sending to people is virtually free! For example, I have a list of previous customers that is over 100,000 strong. I know exactly which customer has purchased which product, which enables me to upsell similar and relevant products and services at the click of a button.

- With the introduction of pay-per-click advertising, new authors and publishers with little or no experience can sell or promote their books straight away.

- Another useful advertising medium is Facebook advertising. For example, I recently promoted an online webinar via Facebook advertising and managed to get over 130 people registered for just £30.

- There are so many different advertising opportunities on the Internet nowadays. For example, you could use an 'affiliate marketing' system to promote your books. This is something that I use to great success within my businesses. I would safely say that at least a third of my business sales come from online affiliates.

- With the Internet there are very few overheads involved. To get started you do not need a flash office or lots of employees. Many people earn in excess of £1,000,000 per year by selling second-hand and new books on eBay! Many of them do this in their spare time.

More and more authors and publishers are using the Internet as a place to advertise and sell because it is fast and easy to use, the number of users is growing every year, your overheads are low, and you don't have to directly interact with the customer.

The basic benefits of E-Commerce

The benefits of e-commerce include:

- Increased sales – this is the first thing that people consider when dealing with e-commerce;

- Decreased costs – your overheads are low;

- Increased profits – due to the fact that your overheads are low;

- The size of your market expands from regional to national or international;

- You can reach a specific target audience through pay-per-click advertising or Facebook ads.

Internet terminology

During the next part of this chapter I will provide you with details of the basic terminology used on the internet. As you progress with your book writing and publishing business, more and more of these terms will become familiar.

URL

Definition: When you go to a web page, the URL of that page is everything that is showing up in the address window of your browser including the http:// and all that comes after it.

Also known as: Uniform Resource Locator or website address.

Domain name

Definition: The main part of the address of a website. This must be purchased and can be used by you if you own it or rent it.

Also known as: Website address or URL.

Tip: When buying a domain name for a website that is being used to promote your book(s), try to purchase one that is relevant to your book category of genre. For example, my books teach the reader 'how to become' a particular career or job; therefore, I decided to buy the domain name www.how2become. com.

Blog or Web Log

Definition: A blog (short for "web log") is a type of web page that serves as a publicly accessible personal journal (or log) for an individual.

Tip: A blog is a great place to promote your book(s). On my website I have a blog which gets updated every week. If you do decide to start a blog, make sure you update it regularly. The major search engines like fresh content and will reward you for this in their rankings. Perhaps the best place to get started with a free blog is www.wordpress.com.

Browse

Definition: To follow links in a page, to shop around in a page exploring what's there, a bit like window shopping. Browsing a web page is different from searching it. When you search a page, you find a search box, enter terms, and find all occurrences of the search term throughout the site. When you browse, you are just clicking around and have to guess which words on the page pertain to your interests. Searching is usually more efficient, but sometimes you find things by browsing that you might not find by searching because you might not think of the "right" term to search for.

Browsers

Definition: Browsers are software programs that enable you to view www documents. They "translate" HTML-encoded files into the text, images, sounds and other features you see.

Cache

Definition: In browsers, a "cache" is used to identify a space where web pages you have visited are stored in your computer. A copy of documents you retrieve is stored in the cache file.

Case sensitive

Definition: Capital letters (upper case) retrieve only upper case. Most search tools are not case sensitive or only respond to initial capitals, as in proper names. It is always safe to key all lower case (no capitals), because lower case will always retrieve upper case.

Cookie

Definition: A message from a web server computer sent to and stored by your browser on your computer. When your computer consults the originating server computer the cookie is sent back to the server, allowing it to respond to you according to the cookie's contents. The main use for cookies is to provide customised web pages according to a profile of your interests. For example, have you ever searched for something online and then that same thing you searched for starts to appear on your screen in the days and weeks after? That's cookie's in action!

Download

Definition: To copy something from a primary source to a more peripheral one, as in saving something found on the web (currently located on a server) to a disk or a file on your local hard drive.

Tip: Consider offering your finished book as a download from your blog or website. I use the Amazon S3 storage facility to store most of my download-able books. You can get a free account here: aws.amazon.com/s3/

Favourites

Definition: In the browser a favourite means to get back to a URL you like, similar to Bookmarks.

Tip: In your book, when drawing people back to your blog or website, try encouraging people to add it to their favourites.

FTP

Definition: File Transfer Protocol. Ability to rapidly transfer entire files from one computer to another intact, for viewing or other purposes.

Host

Definition: A computer that provides web documents to clients or users.

HTML

Definition: Hypertext Markup Language. A standardized language of computer code, embedded in "source" documents behind all web documents, containing the textual content, images, links to other documents (and possibly other applications such as sound or motion), and formatting instructions for display on the screen. When you view a web page you are looking at the product of this code working behind the scenes in conjunction with your browser. Browsers are programmed to interpret HTML for display.

Internet

Definition: The vast collection of interconnected networks that all use the TCP/ IP protocols and that evolved from the ARPANET of the late 60s and early 70s. Note, "internet" (with a lower case "i") refers to any computers that are connected to each other (a network), and are not part of the Internet unless they use TCP/IP protocols. An "intranet" is a private network inside a company or organisation that uses the same kinds of software that you would find on the public internet, but that is only for internal use. An intranet may be on the Internet, or it may simply be a network.

IP Address or IP Number

Definition: (Internet Protocol number or address). A unique number consisting of 4 parts separated by dots, e.g. 165.113.245.2. Every machine that is on the Internet has a unique IP address. If a machine does not have an IP number it is not really on the Internet. Most machines also have one or more Domain Names, which are easier for people to remember.

Purchasing a Web Domain Name

The first step to getting started on the Internet is to purchase and register a domain name. A domain name is the text name corresponding to the numeric IP address of a computer on the Internet. A domain name must be unique. Internet users access your website using your domain name. A domain name is basically the main part of the address of a website. For example, How2become's domain name is: www.how2become.com. You can purchase many different domain names, each with a different 'level' name. For example .com (commercial) is a generic top-level domain (TLD) used on the Internet's Domain Name System. It was one of the original top-level domains, established in January 1985, and has grown to be the largest TLD in use. It is consistently pronounced as a word, dot-com, and has entered the common language in this way. Although .com domains are officially intended to designate commercial entities (others such as government agencies or educational institutions have different top-level domains assigned to them), there has been no restriction on who can register .com domains since the mid-1990s.

I have now indicated other examples of domains that you can purchase.

Examples of domain names:

- .ac.uk - academic (tertiary education and research establishments) and learned societies;
- .co.uk - commercial/general;
- .gov.uk - government (central and local);
- .ltd.uk - limited companies;
- .me.uk - personal;
- .mod.uk - Ministry of Defence and HM Forces public sites;
- .net.uk - ISPs and network companies;
- .nic.uk - network use only;
- .nhs.uk - National Health Service institutions;
- .org.uk - non-profit organisations and charities;
- .plc.uk - public limited companies;
- .police.uk - police forces;
- .sch.uk - schools (primary and secondary education).

The choice of domain name for your book writing and publishing business is totally down to you. One of the important things to remember is that it should be catchy and easy to remember. Try to think of a good name for your website.

Tip: Exact Matching Domains (EMDs) do not have as much weight as they used to in terms of ranking better through natural search engines. An example of an EMD might be an entrepreneur who is selling BOSCH power tools and they decide to buy the domain name www.boschpowertool.co.uk. EMD's used to be very effective at getting lots of traffic through natural search listings, however things have now changed. This does not mean to say you shouldn't have one, but don't rely on it to automatically get you good rankings anymore.

Once you have decided on your domain name you need to see whether it is available to purchase. The Internet has been operating for many years, and you may find that someone has already registered the name you are after.

There have been examples of top tier domain names selling for tens and even hundreds of thousands of pounds. My advice to anyone who is starting out in business is to buy a domain name that is available for a low annual cost. Most .co.uk domain names can be purchased for around £1.99 per year. The .com version of domain names can cost anything up to £10 per year. There are many different web hosting sites where you can search for and purchase domain names.

Here is a list of some of the more commonly used web hosting sites:

www.oneandone.co.uk

www.domainmonster.co.uk

www.reg-123.co.uk

www.webfusion.co.uk

To search for a domain name is simple. Just enter the name of your chosen domain into the search bar on any hosting site and it will tell you if it is available or not.

Hosting

The World Wide Web is a massive collection of websites, all hosted on computers (called web servers) all over the world. The web server (computer) where your website's html files, graphics etc. reside is known as the web host. Web hosting clients simply upload their websites to a shared (or dedicated) web server which the ISP maintains to ensure a constant, fast connection to the Internet. You will find that most domain registration companies will also provide web hosting for you at a low annual fee.

Building a Website

I believe that every author should have either a blog or a website from which to promote their book. Internet traffic is growing every day, which means you could, as a result of this, gain more customers to your site. You can direct customers from your book to your site and keep them informed of all services and products you are selling. Customers can also have easy access to your contact/address details and can be kept up to date of your products and services via a weekly or monthly newsletter.

The biggest decision you will be likely to make is who to get to create your website. You may decide to do it yourself, and there are many web hosting companies such as www.oneandone.co.uk who will provide you with a complete web creation package. I would only recommend you build your own website if you have knowledge of such systems as, speaking from personal experience, it can be extremely frustrating if you don't.

Tip: When getting a website built, I advise that you get it built by a professional – this does not mean you have to pay thousands to get your website built. There are many website services out there where you can also build your own, if you choose to. For example, www.1and1.co.uk allows you to build your own website. Other great websites to visit where you can build your own website include:

www.MoonFruit.com

www.Wix.com

www.GoDaddy.com

www.FatCow.com

If you don't want to try and build a website yourself then consider posting a job on Elance.com or ODesk.com. There are many people on these websites who will design and create a website for you while giving great value for money!

Paying someone else to build your website

There are literally hundreds of companies out there who will create your website for you, all at different costs. If you are going to sell your book via your own website, which I strongly recommend you do, then it is certainly worth considering paying a professional company or individual to do the work for you. However, before you part with your hard-earned cash make sure you ask them questions about the service they can provide. If you are considering writing and publishing a series of books then it might also be worth getting a 'branding session' with the company so that they can get a feel for what type of image you are hoping to portray. For example, when I started my own publishing business I drove all the way up to Northampton to visit the digital design agency Engine Creative (www.enginecreative.co.uk). I asked them to design the 'brand' for my how2become series of books as I had big plans for the publishing business. They ended up creating my logo, website and book cover for me to a very high standard, but they were expensive. In hindsight, I probably paid too much money as a new business start-up, but I wanted to get it right. If I was starting out again I would choose an outsourcer on ODesk.com or Elnace.com to create these for me.

Here are some of the more important questions you may wish to ask a web designer before you agree to a contract:

- What timescale will my website be completed within, and will there be a contract to back this up?
- Are there any 'hidden costs' that I need to take into consideration, such as on-going support or hosting?
- How qualified is the web designer, and can I see some examples of previous work?
- Will he/she keep me updated of any progress? If so, how often will the updates be?
- What is the turnaround time and cost for any future alterations?

Tip: When hiring someone on an outsourcing website to design and build a website for you, I recommend that you create a 'mock up' of the style and functionality you want in a PowerPoint presentation. It is advisable that you spoon-feed the outsourcer so that he or she knows EXACTLY what you want them to do in terms of website design and functionality.

Internet Advertising

Once you have your website built you will want to direct traffic to it in order to generate sales for your book. Traffic is another term for 'visitors' to your website. Don't expect people to find your website just because you have one. You have to go out there and advertise the fact that you have a website, and there are a number of ways in which you can do this:

Search Engines

Major search engine sites such as Google, Bing, MSN and Ask are widely used by internet users. Google accounts for over 70% of all usage and is therefore the most profitable of all the search engines. A search engine does exactly what it says – 'searches'. The user of the site types in a word or phrase and the search engine provides him or her with a number of choices. Some of those choices are provided by the means of natural listings, and the remainder by sponsored links.

Natural Search Listings

Natural search listings are those listings that appear at the discretion of the search engines and that do not incur a charge to the listed site. In most search engines, these are the "main" results.

Search Engine Optimisation

Search Engine Optimisation (SEO) is the process of increasing the amount of visitors to a website by ranking high in the natural search listings of a search engine. The higher a website ranks in the results of a search, the greater the chance that site will be visited by a user. It is common practice for internet users not to click through pages and pages of search results, so a high ranking within the search results is essential for directing more traffic toward the site. SEO helps to ensure that a site is accessible to a search engine and improves the chances that the site will be found by the search engine. Many web developers are skilled in SEO and will be able to provide this service at a cost. An example of a company who specialises in SEO is www.Ayima.com. My advice, especially when starting out as an author, is to generate traffic to your website via either pay-per-click advertising, Facebook adverts, or by simply blogging. Paying a company to promote your website via SEO can be expensive and should only be implemented if your budget allows it, as it can be an expensive and long-term strategy.

However, if you do decide you want to optimise your website for SEO purposes, here is a useful set of websites and services that offer search engine optimisation services.

97th Floor

www.97thfloor.com

Adapt Partners

www.adaptpartners.com

Agillian

www.agillian.com

Ayima

www.Ayima.com

Blind Five Year Old

www.blindfiveyearold.com

Conversion Factory

www.conversionfactory.com

Conversion Rate Experts

www.conversion-rate-experts.com

Distilled

www.distilled.net

EricWard.com

www.ericward.com

High Rankings

www.highrankings.com

iAcquire

www.iacquire.com

Internet Marketing Ninjas

www.internetmarketingninjas.com

Keyphraseology

www.keyphraseology.com

KeyRelevance

www.keyrelevance.com

Page Zero Media

www.pagezero.com

Search Engine College

www.searchenginecollege.com

SEER Interactive

www.seerinteractive.com

SEOgadget

www.seogadget.com

SEOinhouse.com

www.seoinhouse.com

seOverflow

www.seoverflow.com

Squarespace Inc.

www.squarespace.com

Stephan Spencer

www.stephanspencer.com

Techipedia

www.techipedia.com

Trackur

www.trackur.com

User Effect

www.usereffect.com

Vertical Measures

www.verticalmeasures.com

Verve Search

www.vervesearch.com

Tip: There are many companies out there who will offer cost-effective 'link-building' services for your website. Be very careful about employing a company or individual who offers this type of service. Unless you are 100% certain they are genuine and reputable, do not use them. You can easily get penalised by Google for having poor backlinks directed to your website, and sometimes you can even get banned!

To learn more about Search Engine Optimisation and link-building visit www.MOZ.com

Sponsored Links

Sponsored links are basically a form of 'paid advertising' on internet search engines such as Google, Bing or MSN. They are predominantly text based ads appearing at the very top and on the right hand side of search engine results. How far up you appear on the listings of a search engine will be dependent on the search engine's own criteria, how well your adverts perform, and how much you are willing to pay each time somebody clicks on your advert. With pay-per-click advertising you create your own ads and choose key-words, which are words or phrases related to your business. With regards to advertising for a book, you will need to be very careful that you only target keywords or phrases that are highly relevant to your book subject. For example, I currently use pay-per-click advertising to promote a book which is called 'firefighter interview questions and answers'. When using pay-per-click to promote this book I will only bid on the following keywords and phrases:

- Firefighter interview tips

- Firefighter interview questions

- Firefighter interview questions and answers

- Firefighter interview sample interview questions

- Firefighter interview helps

Through continuous testing and experience I have found that keywords and phrases that are highly relevant to my book subject matter will convert into sales. Anything else will simply bot convert!

When people search on a search engine using one of your keywords your ad may appear next to the search results. The beauty of this method is that you are now advertising to an audience that's already interested in your business. People can simply click your ad to learn more about you and your book, and hopefully make a purchase.

The problem you have to overcome with this method is getting people to actually buy your product after they have clicked through to your site. You will now hopefully understand why I encourage you to sell your book(s) on Amazon, simply because it is FREE traffic!

SPONSORED LINKS TIPS AND ADVICE

Make sure your adverts are relevant

By this I mean make sure that your adverts are relevant to the words and phrases you are bidding on.

For example, if you are selling a book that teaches people how to open a restaurant you would not want to bid on the phrase 'local restaurants'. Instead you would want to bid on keyword phrases such as 'setting up a restaurant' or 'how to open a restaurant' etc. A good strategy used by many experienced pay-per-click advertisers is to match the main heading of the advert with the phrase or keyword you are bidding on. By doing this you are more likely to increase your click through rate and therefore get more traffic to your site for less money.

Test the market first

If you decide to sell your book via internet search engines, make sure you test the market before you start spending hundreds of pounds on your advertising campaigns.

One of the biggest mistakes people make when advertising through spon- sored links is that they waste money when starting out. They want their ads to be right at the top of the tree and are prepared to pay heavily for it. It is far better to bid at a low price initially and test your adverts to see if they create a good 'click through rate'. If the click through rate is good and you are not selling anything then you may need to make some changes to either your book or your website in order to change this situation. Do not bid high prices on your adverts either, as you need to factor in your costs for printing the book and also for leaving a decent margin for yourself. It is pointless spending £8 on advertising for every book that you sell for £10 as you would be losing money once you have factored in your printing costs! Start your bids very low, and only increase them once you know that your book sells.

AFFILIATE MARKETING

Affiliate Marketing is one of the most effective methods for selling your book online. In a nutshell, affiliate marketing is where people sell your book online in exchange for a 'commission' per sale that they make. The commission rate will vary, and it will normally be paid as a percentage of the recommended retail price or a set fee per unit sale. For example, on my website www. how2become.com I pay up to 45% commission to my affiliates for every product they sell. As an example, if one of my affiliates sells a book for me at £15, they would receive £6.75 in commission.

INTERNET MARKETING - GLOSSARY OF USEFUL TERMS

301 Redirect – A 301 redirect automatically causes one URL to redirect to another and tells the Web (and search engines) that this redirect is perma- nent, as opposed to a temporary (302) redirect. 301 redirects are generally preferable for Search Engine Optimization purposes and are therefore often referred to as search engine friendly redirects.

Above the Fold – The part of the page you can see without scrolling down or over. The exact amount of space will vary by viewer because of screen settings. You often pay a premium for advertisement placements above the fold, which will add to the costs of internet marketing services, but it may also add to results.

Advertising Network – A group of websites where one advertiser controls all or a portion of the ads for all sites. A common example is the Google Search Network, which includes AOL, Amazon, Ask.com (formerly Ask Jeeves), and thousands of other sites. In Google AdWords they offer two types of ad networks on the Internet; search and display (which used to be called their content network).

Google AdWords – AdWords is Google's paid search marketing program, the largest such program in the world, and it is in most countries with notable exceptions such as China (Baidu) and Russia (Yandex). Introduced in 2001, AdWords was the first pay-per-click provider offering the concept of a Quality Score, which factors search relevancy (via click-through rate) in along with a bid to determine ad position.

Affiliate Marketing – A type of internet marketing in which you partner with other websites, individuals, or companies to send traffic to your site. You will typically pay on a Cost per Acquisition (CPA) or Cost per Click (CPC) basis.

Algorithm – The term search engines use for the formulae that determine the rankings of your Natural Listings. Search Engines will periodically send a Spider through your Website to view all its information. Their programs then analyse this and other data to rate your site and to decide whether or not it will appear in response to specific searches, and if so how high or low on the page it will come. These algorithms can be very complicated (Google alone currently uses 106 different variables), and search engines closely guard their algorithms as trade secrets.

ALT Tags – HTML tags used to describe website graphics by displaying a block of text when moused-over. Search Engines are generally unable to view graphics or distinguish text that might be contained within them, and the implementation of an ALT tag enables Search Engines to categorise that graphic. There is also talk that business websites will be required to utilize ALT tags for all pictures in order to comply with certain American Disability Act requirements.

Google Analytics– Also known as Web Metrics. Analytics refers to a collection of data about a website and its users. Analytics programs typically give performance data on clicks, time, pages viewed, website paths, and a variety of other information. The proper use of web analytics allows website owners to improve their visitor experience, which often leads to higher ROI tor profit-based sites.

Anchor Text – The clickable words of a hypertext link; they will appear as the underlined blue part in standard web design. In the preceding sentence, "hypertext link" is the anchor text. As with anything in SEO it can be overdone, but generally speaking using your important keywords in the anchor text is highly desirable.

Backlinks– Links from other websites pointing to any particular page on your site. Search Engines use backlinks to judge a site's credibility; if a site links to you, the reasoning goes, it is in effect vouching for your authority on a particular subject. Therefore, Link Building is an incredibly important part of Search Engine Optimisation. How many links, the quality of the sites linking to you, and how they link to you are all important factors.

Banners – Picture advertisements placed on websites. Such advertising is a staple of internet marketing branding campaigns. Depending upon their size and shape, banner ads may also be referred to as buttons, inlines, leaderboards, skyscrapers, or other terms. Specifically, banner ads refer to a 468×60 pixel size. Banner ads can be static pictures, animated, or interactive. Banner ads appear anywhere on a site – top, middle, bottom, or either side. Banner costs vary by website and advertiser; two of the most popular pay structures are Cost per 1,000 Impressions (CPM) and flat costs for a specified period of time.

Black Hat SEO – The opposite of White Hat SEO, these Search Engine Optimization (or 'SEO') tactics are (attempted) ways of tricking the Search Engines to get better rankings for a website. If not immediately, using black hat methods will eventually get your site drastically lower rankings or banned from the search engines altogether. While there are completely legal and ethical techniques you can use to improve rankings, if you design and market a website mostly for humans and not for the Search Engines' Spiders you should be okay.

Blog – Short for web log, blogs are part journal, part website. Typically the newest entry (blog post) appears at the top of the page, with older entries following in reverse chronological order. As mentioned previously, several blogging platforms exist and my personal favourite is WordPress.com.

Click through Rate (CTR) – # of clicks / # of impressions. Click through rate is a common internet marketing measurement tool for ad effectiveness. This rate tells you how many times people are actually clicking on your ad out of the number of times your ad is shown. Low click through rates can be caused by a number of factors, including copy, placement, and relevance.

Cloaking – Showing a Search Engine Spider or bot one version of a web page and a different version to the end user. Several Search Engines have explicit rules against unapproved cloaking. Those violating these guidelines may find their pages penalised or banned from a Search Engine's index. As for approved cloaking, this generally only happens with Search Engines that offer a paid inclusion program. Anyone offering cloaking services should be able to demonstrate explicit approval from a search engine for what they intend to do.

Content Management System – Content Management Systems (CMS) allow website owners to make text and picture changes to their websites without specialised programming knowledge of software like Adobe Dreamweaver or Microsoft FrontPage. Content Management Systems can be edited by anyone with basic word knowledge via an internet connection. There is no need for lengthy or costly web development contracts or to wait for someone outside your company to make changes. CMS examples include WordPress, Drupal, and Joomla.

Conversion Rate – This statistic, or metric, tells you what percentage of people is converting (really!) The definition of "conversion" depends upon your goals and measurements. It could mean a sign up for free information, a completed survey, a purchase made, or any other target set by you.

Cookie – Think of cookies like Batman's Bat Tracer. When you visit a web-site, Batman sticks a cookie on your browser to follow you around. Batman can then go back to his Bat Cave and watch where you're going and where you've been. A little Big Brother-ish to be sure, but cookies also provide direct benefits to surfers, including remembering passwords and bringing you offers in which you are genuinely interested.

Cost per Acquisition (CPA) – An online advertising cost structure where you pay per an agreed upon actionable event, such as a lead, registration, or sale.

Cost per Click (CPC) – A common way to pay for Search Engine and other types of online advertising, CPC means you pay a pre-determined amount each time someone clicks on your advertisement to visit your site. You usually set a top amount you are willing to pay per click for each search term, and the amount you pay will be equal to or less than that amount, depending on the particular Search Engine and your competitors' bids. This is also referred to as Pay-Per-Click (PPC) or Paid Search Marketing.

Cost per Impression (CPM) – A common internet marketing cost structure, especially for banner advertising. You agree to pay a set cost for every 1,000 impressions your ad receives. Search engine marketing may involve CPM costs for Contextual Advertising. This internet advertising pay structure should really be called Cost per 1,000 Impressions.

Crawler – Component of a Search Engine that gathers listings by automatically "crawling" the Web. A search engine's crawler (also known as a Spider or robot) follows links to web pages. It makes copies of those pages and stores them in a Search Engine's index.

CSS – CSS is short for Cascading Style Sheet – it is a way to move style elements off individual web pages and sites to allow for faster loading pages, smaller file sizes, and other benefits for visitors, search engines, and designers.

Customer Relationship Management (CRM) – Software solutions that help enterprise businesses manage customer relationships in an organised way. An example of a CRM would be a database containing detailed customer information that management and salespeople can reference in order to match customer needs with products and inform customers of service requirements, etc.

Description Tags – HTML tags which provide a brief description of your site that Search Engines can understand. Description tags should contain the main keywords of the page it is describing in a short summary – don't go crazy here with Keyword Stuffing.

Directories – A type of Search Engine where listings are gathered through human efforts rather than web crawling. In directories websites are often reviewed, summarised to a brief description, and placed in a relevant category.

Domain Name – A website's main address.

EdgeRank – The algorithm Facebook uses to rank a page's or profile's posts to determine which of those posts will appear in the newsfeeds of users connected to those pages and profiles (or pages and profiles tagged in the posts). The higher an EdgeRank, the more likely you will appear in the newsfeeds. Facebook does not release this data publicly for either the pages or individual posts.

Email Campaign System – Email is perhaps the most overlooked and underutilized (based on cost and effectiveness) form of internet marketing today. Email campaign systems allow organizations to send out emails to their email lists with a standard look and feel. Features often include the ability to segment lists.

Feed – An XML language that uses either RSS or Atom formatting is an extremely popular way for organizations to get their messages through the clutter and into the hands of interested parties. With the simple click of an orange button (right), users can stay connected to a site's content (Blogs, news, podcasts, etc.) automatically anytime their computers are connected to the Internet. That button will connect you to the feed for the Found Blog.

Forum – A place on the Internet where people with common interests or backgrounds come together to find information and discuss topics.

Google AdWords Certified Partner – Google AdWords offers the most extensive certification process of any of the paid search marketing providers. The Google AdWords Certified Partner program replaces the earlier Qualified Google Advertising Company/Individual program.

Header (or Heading) Tags () – HTML heading and subheading tags are critical components of Search Engine marketing, as often times both are graphical and thereby unreadable to Search Engine Spiders. Optimally, page titles should also be included to clearly define the page's purpose and theme. All of the header tags should be used according to their relevance, with more prominent titles utilizing <h1>, subheaders using <h2>, and so on.

HTML– HyperText Markup Language, the programming language used in websites. Developers use other languages that can be read and understood by HTML to expand what they can do on the Web.

Hyperlink – Often blue and underlined, hyperlinks, commonly called "links" for short, allow you to navigate to other pages on the Web with a simple click of your mouse.

Image Maps – Clickable regions on images that make links more visually appealing and websites more interesting. Image maps enable Spiders to "read" this material.

Impressions – The number of times someone views a page displaying your ad. Note that this is not the same as actually seeing your ad, making placement and an understanding of the site's traffic particularly important when paying on a Cost per 1,000 Impressions basis.

Inbound or Incoming Links – See Backlinks

Index – The collection of information a Search Engine has that searchers can query against. With crawler-based Search Engines the index is typically made up of copies of all the web pages they have found from crawling the Internet. With human-powered directories the index contains the summaries of all the websites that have been categorized.

Internal Linking – Placing hyperlinks on a page leading to other pages within the same site. This helps users to find more information, improve site inter-action, and enhances your SEO efforts.

JavaScript – Not to be confused with its distant cousin Java – this is an Object Oriented Programming language developed by NetScape. It is used primarily to improve user experiences on websites with enhanced functionality.

Keyword – Almost interchangeable with Search Term, Keywords are words or a group of words that a person may search for in a Search Engine. Key-words also refer to the terms you bid on through Search Engine marketing in trying to attract visitors to your website or Landing Page. Part of successful Search Engine Optimization is including Keywords in your website copy and Meta Tags.

Keyword Stuffing – When the Web was young and Search Engines were starting to gain in popularity, some smart website owners realized that the Search Engine Algorithms really liked some Meta Tags. So they started stuffing a bunch of Keywords, often with high search volumes and no rele-vancy to the site, into title, description, and Keyword Tags. Sites instantly rocketed to great SERPs. Soon thereafter the Search Engines changed their ranking formulae, and the sites lost their positions or were banned outright.

Keyword Tags – HTML tags which define the Keywords used on web pages. Meta Keyword Tags used to carry great weight with some older Search Engines until they caught up with the spammers using this practice and modified their algorithms. Today Google is officially on record for not giving these tags any weight.

Landing Page – The first page a person sees when coming to your website from an advertisement. This page can be any page on your website, including your home page. Almost any time you direct someone to your website from an advertisement you should send them to a specialized landing page with tailored information to increase your landing page Conversion Rate. Radio advertisements are a notable exception, as spelling out specific URL's can be time consuming and difficult to remember. Direct Online Marketing™ has extensive experience in creating, testing, and modifying landing page conversion rates to give your business the highest quality, least expensive, most cost effective leads possible.

Link Building – The process of obtaining Hyperlinks (links) from websites back to yours. Link Building is a crucial part of Search Engine Optimisation.

Link Popularity – How many websites link to yours, how popular those linking sites are, and how much their content relates to yours. Link popularity is an important part of Search Engine Optimization, which also values the sites that you link out to.

Local Business Listings – Each of the major Search Engines offer local business listings that appear next to maps at the top of the page on many locally targeted searches. Business may either submit new requests or claim existing local business listings if the Search Engines have already added the company to the results. Having a website is not required for having a local business listing.

Long Tail Keywords – Rather than targeting the most common Keywords in your industry, you can focus on more niche terms that are usually longer phrases but are also easier and quicker to rank for in the Search Engines. Long Tail Keywords can amount to as much as 60% or more of a site's search traffic.

Meta Tags (see also keyword tags, description tags etc.) – Meta Tags allow you to highlight important Keywords related to your site in a way that matters to Search Engines, but that your website visitors typically do not see. Meta Tags have risen and fallen in terms of valuation by internet marketers and Search Engines alike (see Keyword Stuffing), but they still play an important role in Search Engine Optimization. Examples of Meta Tags include Header Tags and Alt Tags.

Microblogging – Microblogging refers to platforms allowing you to post information in snippets of 140 characters at a time via phone or web. Twitter quickly became the dominant global player, to the point where its name is synonymous with Microblogging. In China, however, there are other popular Microblogging services, generically called weibo.

Mobile Marketing – As cell phone technology advances advertisers can reach their target audience virtually anywhere. While Mobile Marketing is really just an extension of online marketing, it provides businesses with many new opportunities and challenges. How does your website look on your Blackberry or Treo?

Natural Listings – Also referred to as "organic results", the non-advertised listings in Search Engines. Some Search Engines may charge a fee to be included in their Natural Listings, although most are free. How high or low your website is ranked depends on many factors, two of the most important being content relevance and Link Popularity.

Opt-in – This type of registration requires a person submitting information to specifically request he or she be contacted or added to a list. Opt-ins typically lower lead flow rates and raise Costs per Acquisition from internet marketing campaigns, but they may produce a higher percentage of interested leads.

Opt-out – Here people are automatically signed up to receive contact, but they can opt out of receiving newsletters, calls, etc. at any time.

Organic Listings – See Natural Listings.

Outbound Links – Links on any web page leading to another web page, whether they are within the same site or another website.

PageRank – PageRank is a value that Google assigns for pages and web-sites that it indexes based on all of the factors in its algorithm. Google does release an external PageRank, scoring pages from 1-10 that you can check for any website, but this external number is not the same as the internal PageRank Google uses to determine Search Engine results. All independent Search Engines have their own version of PageRank. Potentially interesting fact: PageRank was named for Google's Larry Page and it is calculated at the page level.

Paid Listings – Listings that Search Engines sell to advertisers, usually through paid placement or paid inclusion programs. In contrast, organic (Natural) Listings are not sold.

Pay Per Click (PPC) – See Cost per Click (CPC), above. The most common type of Search Engine advertising cost structure is PPC Search Engine marketing. Google, Yahoo, MSN, and many more Search Engines all use PPC.

Pop-Up – An extremely abused type of online marketing advertisement, Pop-Ups open new windows on your screen that partially or wholly cover your current Web Browser window. Some Search Engines ban ads that create a certain number (or even any) Pop-Up ads. Direct Online Marketing™ does not include Pop-Ups or pop-unders as part of its internet marketing services.

Query – Query is another term for "Keyword" or "search term." Within Google AdWords, search query reports show the actual terms that searchers used to click on your ads as opposed to the advertised Keyword that is in your account. These two sets of words may or may not be the same.

Rank – How well a particular web page or website is listed in the Search Engine's results. For example, a web page about apples may be listed in response to a Query for "apples." However, "Rank" indicates where exactly it was listed – be it on the first page of results, the second page or perhaps the 200th page. Alternatively, it might also be said to be ranked first among all the results, or 12th, or 111th. Overall, saying a page is "listed" only means that it can be found within a Search Engine in response to a Query, not that it necessarily ranks well for that query. Rank is also known as 'position'.

Real Simple Syndication (RSS) – An increasingly popular new technology that allows information to be easily shared on websites or given directly to users per their request. Click here for a feed to the Official Direct Online Marketing™ Blog. RSS feeds create new online advertising opportunities, although marketers are still debating how best to use them.

Reciprocal Link – A link exchange between two sites. Both sites will display a link to the other site somewhere on their pages. This type of link is generally much less desirable than a one-way inbound link.

Remarketing – Remarketing is Google AdWords's term for retargeting.

Results Page – Also referred to as a Search Engine Results Page.

Return on Investment (ROI) – The key statistic for many companies; are your advertisements generating a profit, and if so, how much profit compared with the money you have had to pay out? Direct Online Marketing™ always has its eye on ROI for all partners…and you should, too!

Rich Media – Web advertisements or pages that are more animated and/or interactive than static Banners or pages.

Robot or Bot – See Crawler.

Robots.txt – A file used to keep web pages from being indexed or to tell which pages you want a Search Engine to index.

Scraping – The process of copying content from one web property and using it on another. In other words, stealing. Scraping technologies have evolved because of the need for content and to stay ahead of legitimate content creators trying to protect what they've written. Some companies offer content monitoring to help protect against Scraping.

Search Engines – Search Engines are places people go to search for things on the Internet, such as Yahoo!, Google, or Bing. Most Search Engines provide websites with two ways of appearing: Natural (free) and Paid. Natural Listings, also referred to as organic listings, appear based on the Search Engines' own formulae. You can't pay to have your site listed higher (although some Search Engines require that you pay to be included in the Natural Listings), but you can perform Search Engine Optimization (SEO). Paid Listings usually appear above or to the side of natural listings and are typically identifiable as advertisements. The most common cost for advertising on Paid Listings through paid search is Pay-Per-Click (PPC).

Search Engine Optimization (SEO) – A fancy way of saying "making your site Search Engine friendly". Search Engine Optimization is typically difficult to do on your own, especially given the increasing complexity and differences among all the Search Engines. Two important factors that rank highly in all major Search Engines are Link Popularity (how many websites – and how highly ranked those sites are – link to you) and relevant content (how pertinent information on your website or a particular web page is to a search).

Search Engine Results Page – Search Engine Results Pages, or SERPs, are the web pages displayed by any Search Engine for any given search. They display both Natural (organic) Listings and Pay-Per-Click ads. How high you are listed and where your ad is shown depends on Search Engine Optimization and paid Search Engine Marketing respectively.

Search Terms – A Search Term is a word or group of words that a person types into a Search Engine to find what they are looking for. Based upon what a company sells, a website should incorporate the most popular or most popular specific Search Terms into the copy as Keywords. Figuring out the appropriate Search Terms to put into a website and to advertise on is a huge part of a Search Engine Marketer's job.

Social Commerce - Selling goods directly online through social media channels. Just like "electronic commerce" was shortened to "ecommerce", social commerce is sometimes shortened to "s-commerce" or "f-commerce," the latter being short for "Facebook commerce."

Social Media - A type of online media where information is primarily uploaded through user submission. Web surfers are no longer simply consumers of content, they are now active content publishers. Many different forms of Social Media exist, including more established formats like Forum and Blogs and newer formats like Wikis, podcasts, Social Networking, image and video sharing, and virtual reality.

Spam – Can refer to unwanted data sent via email or put on a website to game a Search Engine. You're probably aware of spam in the classic email sense, and hopefully also aware of the strict standards and penalties associated with the CAN-SPAM Act. Spam to a Search Engine is web content that the Search Engine deems to be detrimental to its efforts to deliver relevant, quality search results. Some Search Engines have written guidelines about what they consider to be spamming, but ultimately any activity a Search Engine deems harmful may be considered Spam, regardless of whether or not there are published guidelines against it.

Spider – A noun and a verb, Search Engines have Spiders crawl through all the linked pages of a website to gather information to include the site in their Natural Listings, and it is also used to determine their ranking on various Search Terms.

Stickiness – How often people return to a website. Constant updates, news feeds, and exclusive content are all ways to make a site stickier.

Tags – Words or phrases used to describe and categorize individual blog posts, videos, and pictures. Correctly using Tags organizes content for users and can help with visibility through SEO and Social Media optimisation.

Text Ad – An online advertisement that contains only written copy. Paid listings found on the results pages of the main Search Engines are currently Text Ads, although this is starting to change. Soon you should expect to see video ads pop up here occasionally.

TLD – TLD stands for Top Level Domain. The TLD is determined by whatever comes at the end of a domain name at its root – meaning without any page names. So for example, the TLD for our site, www.directom.com, is ".com."

Tracking Code – Information typically included in the URL that allows an advertiser to track the effectiveness of various aspects of an advertisement.

URL – Uniform Resource Locator. These are the letters and symbols that make up the address of specific web pages.

Viral Marketing – A newer method of internet marketing that attempts to make advertisements so interesting that viewers will pass them along to others free of charge to the advertisers.

Web Browser – The program you use to access the Internet. Common browsers include Microsoft Internet Explorer (IE), Apple's Safari, and Mozilla Firefox.

Webinar – "Web Seminar". These virtual seminars allow people from anywhere in the world to attend via an internet connection. They offer tremendous opportunities for businesses to reach out to people over large geographic areas at low costs.

White Hat SEO – Used to describe certain Search Engine Optimization (SEO) methods. Being "White Hat" means using only SEO techniques that are completely above board and accepted by the Search Engines. Doing the opposite (Black Hat) can lead to your website seeing its rankings drop drastically – or being banned altogether – even if the Search Engine Optimization tactics aren't currently banned by Search Engines.

Wiki – A user-written, controlled, and edited site. Anyone with web access can change information appearing on Wikis, which can be about broad or specific topics. Wikis are becoming increasingly popular websites as people search for quality and (hopefully) unbiased information. The best known example is Wikipedia.

WordPress – WordPress is an extremely popular Content Management System. Developed originally for blogs, WordPress offers a great degree of flexibility and functionality.

XML – Extensible Markup Language. Content developers use this language with a variety of forms of content, including text, audio, and visual, in order to allow users to define their own elements and pull the data at their pace. XML has played a huge part in the transformation of the Web towards Web 2.0.

CHAPTER 16

ALTERNATIVE WAYS TO MARKET AND PROMOTE YOUR BOOK

Get instant access to over 32 hours' worth of online training videos and support at:

www.BookPublishingAcademy.co.uk

ALTERNATIVE WAYS TO MARKET AND PROMOTE YOUR BOOK

In this next section of the guide I will provide you with a number of useful methods for promoting and marketing your book. I have personally found that all of these methods have worked for me over the years, and you may decide to choose one or a number of them when developing and growing your own writing and publishing business.

Building a list or database to promote your books and other products or services to

This has to be one of the most powerful methods for growing your business. At the time of writing I have a list of over 100,000 previous customers. This means that I have the power to contact all of them whenever I want in order to sell them my latest books and training courses. The only slight drawback with this method is that people tend to change their email addresses, and a certain portion of my list will inevitably be outdated. However, if you constantly try to 'build' your list you will have a stream of new people to promote your books and products to.

In order to build a list you will need an appropriate service or piece of software which enables you to capture people's names and email addresses on your website. There are many different types of services that will provide this kind of service, however I personally find that **www.marketerschoice.co.uk** is an exceptional marketing tool for this purpose, and I know that many other successful entrepreneurs have found this to be great, too. You can get a free trial of marketerschoice by visiting their website, and they also have some easy-to-follow video tutorials which will enable you to implement some of their excellent tools. Whilst the system is primarily a shopping cart to be used on an ecommerce website, they do allow you to build a list and contact that list as many times as you wish.

On many of my websites I use what is called an 'opt-in' field in order to capture people's details. Once I have their details it is then down to me to turn them into a paying customer. An opt-in is basically a piece of website code which I place on my website – this code allows people to enter their details and in return they will receive something from me in return; usually a free chapter of my book. Once I have their details I can then contact them at any time in the future to offer them books and courses which are relevant to their needs. I can either contact them by sending a 'broadcast' email whenever I have a new book to offer or by a series of autoresponders which are set up to be sent to that person after a set number of days have passed since they opted in. The autoresponder system means that I only have to write the email once and it will then get sent to each person who 'opts in' after a set number of days (determined by me) has passed.

In order to make this a little clearer, I have created the two-step plan below which details what will happen after 'Steve' enters his name and email address into the relevant opt-in fields on my website:

STEP 1 – Steve opts in to my website after I offer to send him a free chapter of my book. Steve has visited a page on my website that offers free interview advice. In order to tempt him to opt-in, I will offer him a free chapter of my latest interview skills book.

STEP 2 - As soon as he enters his name and email address into the sample box below, the autoresponder will then send him an email which contains a link where he can download the free chapter. I will usually upload the free to chapter to my Amazon S3 account.

Sample opt-in box where Steve enters his details:

Join the XYZ list name now and you'll receive_

"The title of your offer goes here"

Your Name: [   ]
Your Email: [   ]

SEND ME MY FREE CHAPTER NOW!

The email Steve will receive after he has entered his details into the box above:

Dear Steve,

Hi, it's Richard McMunn here. Thanks for joining my newsletter!

As promised, you can download the FREE chapter of my latest interview skills book at the link below:

PLACE THE AMAZON S3 DOWNLOAD LINK HERE TO YOUR FREE BOOK CHAPTER

I will periodically send you information and details in the future that will help you to grow and develop your business.

In the meantime, if you have any questions, please don't hesitate to contact me.

Kind regards

Richard McMunn

- **Address will go here.**
- **A link for people to unsubscribe will go here.**

A couple of things to note about autoresponders and broadcasts:

o You should limit the number of times you contact your list of subscribers to a maximum of 2 per week. If you do any more than this you will start to see more and more people 'unsubscribe'.

o Be sure to only offer your list products and services which are relevant to what they have opted into and which are of a high quality.

o NEVER spam your list.

o You should try sending your list or database free products, services, information or incentives. The main aim of your list is to build trust so that the people who have opted-in will eventually buy your books(s) from you. I have found that people will generally buy from me after the seventh communication or autoresponder – it can take a lot of effort to build trust, and this can be done by offering your customers free and valuable information and by making sure that your contact details and address are at the bottom of the email.

o The majority of shopping carts and email autoresponder tools will enable you to personalise the emails, broadcasts and autoreponders you set up. For example, in the email template to 'Steve' you will notice that his name has been entered at the top of the email – 'Dear Steve'. If you personalise the email the person receiving it will be far more likely to read it.

o You should also consider adding their name into the subject header of the message you are sending. Put yourself in the shoes of the recipient – they probably receive many emails a day, and it is your job to make them open the email. You can do this by both adding their name into the subject heading and also by asking them a question. Here's an example of the subject email heading to get Steve to open the email and download the business plan template:

Steve, you can download your interview skills chapter here.

And here's a few more great examples of email subject headings that will entice people to open them:

Steve, here's 10 important tips to help you pass your interview.

Steve, do you want to triple your chances of passing your next interview?

You should try and be creative with your emails, but never put the word 'FREE' in the subject heading and limit the number of times you use it in the actual content of the email – email inboxes are becoming increasingly more sophisticated and will place some emails they deem to be 'marketing' in the spam folder. If your email goes into someone's spam folder they will probably never open it!

Although I have mentioned **www.marketerschoice.co.uk** as my chosen shopping cart and autoresponder system, there are still many other great ways to do the same thing. In no particular order, here's a few more that you should check out:

- Awebber
- Infusionsoft
- Mailchimp

Newspaper and local media advertising

We are undoubtedly living in changing times, and fewer people are buying and reading newspapers, especially local ones! However, these can still be effective ways to test a book which you want to offer your customers. Here are a few important tips to consider when advertising in local or national printed newspapers:

- DO NOT pay the rate card price for the size advert you want. There are massive discounts to be had, especially a day or two before the paper goes to print. If there is advertising space left close to the print deadline then you can get at least 50% off the rate card. When dealing with sales teams from local and national newspapers, be sure to barter hard on the price.

- Unless the price you are paying for advertising space in local or national press is very cheap you should always insist on your advert being placed on the right hand page of the newspaper or magazine. Your advert will get more exposure on the right hand side of a page, simply because the way people read and scan newspapers naturally draws people to the right. Strange, but true!

- When writing or creating your advert for the newspaper I strongly recommend you include a 'call to action'. A call to action is basically telling the reader of the advert to take some form of action, examples being:

- Asking them to visit your website to download a FREE chapter of your new book.

- Asking them to complete a form and send it back to you in exchange for some type of incentive.

- Visit your website or business in order to get a discount if they quote a specific reference name or number when buying your book.

Advertising using social media such as Facebook and Twitter

Social media advertising can be a very effective method to use for authors and self-publishers. Facebook and Twitter will allow you to pay for adverts that are placed right under the noses of your target audience. However, the difference between advertising on Facebook or Twitter, as opposed to my preferred method of using Pay-Per-Click advertising (detailed next), is that people are not necessarily 'searching' for your product. This means you have to work harder to get a sale or conversion from social media advertising, whereas people searching via Google and other prominent search engines are more likely to be looking to buy your book or service.

The benefits of using Facebook, Twitter, Pinterest and other social media channels as an author and self-publisher are as follows:

- It is a free form of advertising if you choose not to pay for adverts.
- It allows you to build trust with your readers.
- It gives you the tools to promote new books and services.
- It allows you to build up a big following relatively quickly.

Whilst there are many benefits to using social media as a way to generate leads and sales for your book writing and publishing business, there are pitfalls to be aware of too:

- It can be harder to generate sales via social media.
- If people are unhappy with your service they have the option to tell everyone on Facebook. (Whilst this is a pitfall, it can work to your advantage as it will force you to offer great products and customer service.
- Once you start using social media you MUST keep the pages and posts updated. If your page has been inactive for some time it can deter people from interacting with you or buying your book(s).
- There are many companies and websites out there offering you to 'buy' Facebook likes and Twitter followers. My advice is to avoid these at all costs. You should build your follows organically and by keeping your page engaging and interesting.

A great way to get more Facebook likes and Twitter followers is to create a competition on your page and Twitter feed. For example, let's assume you are going to be launching your new book in just 4 weeks' time and you want to start creating a buzz around it. A great way to build 'likes' and followers is to offer people the chance to win a signed copy of your new book if they like your Facebook page or follow you on Twitter. In order to get the most from this type of campaign you should make a post on your page or feed and encourage people to 'share' the competition with their friends. I have known of some competitions going viral, so this is a great way to build a list of followers via social media for your business.

More about pay-per-click advertising to generate book sales

Undoubtedly, for me, this has to be one of the most effective methods for generating leads and book sales. The problem for many people who have no experience in using it is tackling the maze that is Adwords. If you get it wrong it will cost you dearly. Get it right, and you are certainly onto a winner.

Pay-per-click (PPC) advertising was first introduced by Yahoo.com back in the early 2000's. It was an idea that would revolutionise advertising and the way that we use the Internet to search for the things that we want. Although Yahoo.com were the first 'smart cookies' to introduce PPC advertising, it was Google who really dominated the market by making their systems both highly effective and functional, but also relevant to what people were searching for – and this still stands true today.

'Relevance' is the key to PPC advertising, and Google certainly got this part right. The latest figures distributed reveal that over 70% of traffic searches are handled by Google. The remainder of traffic is spread about amongst the other search engine sites such as Bing, Ask and MSN. How the board members at Yahoo must now be kicking themselves for not dominating their own idea!

Anyway, what makes all of this great for you as an author and publisher is that you can get literally hundreds of 'relevant' visitors to your website within seconds. Of course, there are a number of pitfalls when using PPC advertising, but if you take the time to learn the system then you can generate a lot of sales in the process.

Earlier on I mentioned the word 'relevance'. Relevance is not only crucial to your advertising campaigns, it is also crucial to how many books you will sell from your website or blog at a profit. Here's why:

Keyword searches

People who search for goods or information online will type a word or a phrase into the search engine. Once they click 'search' they will be provided with hundreds, thousands, and sometimes millions of pages of 'relevant' websites. These websites are provided in order of most relevance, and Google will use its unique PageRank system to achieve this. The websites that appear on the natural rankings of Google get most of the traffic for free, therefore there is a great incentive to get your website to appear on these free rankings. The only problem is that nobody, and I mean nobody, knows how Google's algorithm actually works, with the obvious exception of Google themselves.

Taking into account all of the above information, it is vitally important that you choose your 'keywords and phrases' very carefully. In addition to the natural search rankings that Google creates you will also notice that there are a number of 'sponsored results' at the very top of the page and on the right hand side of the search engine page. These are what are called 'paid for advertising', or PPC as we better know them.

PPC does exactly what it says on the tin. Every time a person clicks on your advert, you have to pay for it, regardless of whether they buy anything or not! Therefore, there's a lot more to online advertising than simply getting traffic to your website, as there's also the art of conversion to consider, too. In very basic terms, you will decide how much you are prepared to pay every time a person clicks through your advert. Because you are going to be selling a book, which may retail between £10 and £15, you will probably want to bid something like £0.10 - £0.20 per click.

Now here's the trick. In order to pay less for your adverts and each time a person clicks through on it, you MUST make your advert relevant to what people are searching for. This can be achieved in a number of ways:

1. Choose a domain name that matches, or is similar to, the search term. These are more commonly referred to as Exact matching Domains, or EMD's. Although EMD's are not beneficial to natural search engine rankings any longer, they can still work quite well for PPC advertising.

2. Make sure you include the search term in your advert - Google will make relevant domains and search terms bold so that they stand out.

3. Use 'capitalisation' in your adverts with the terms of Google's advertising policies. Again, these will allow the advert to stand out from the rest.

The more your advert stands out from the rest, the more people will click through on it. Because Google is so hell-bent on providing its users with relevant content, it will charge you less the more people who 'click through' on your advert (Click Through Rate - CTR). If more people are clicking through on your advert, then it must mean your website is relevant to the search term! Bingo, everyone's a winner!

In order to help you get the most from PPC advertising, here are a few great tips:

- **Paying a company to set up your PPC campaign** - It is worth considering paying a professional company to set up your campaign for you if your budget will stretch this far. The reason for this is that you can end up wasting lots of money on clicks that will not convert, and a professional company will be able to test your adverts and keywords for you. Although I am not endorsing this company, I have used **www.nutpog.com** on more than one occasion to set up my PPC campaigns. I do appreciate however that most authors will only have one book to sell, and as such paying a company to set up your PPC account will not be financially viable.

- **Set your advertising budget low to begin with** - When you start advertising using PPC I recommend you set your daily budget quite low. This will allow you to test the market and see whether or not your book actually converts into a sale. If you are getting lots of visitors to your website but none of them are buying or interacting, then there may be an issue with your website or sales-page.

- **Add negative keywords to your campaign** - Negative keywords can help you to reach the most interested customers, reduce your costs, and increase your return on investment (ROI). When you add negative keywords your ad won't show to people searching for those terms or visiting sites that contain those terms. With negative keywords, you can:

- Prevent your ad from showing to people searching for or visiting websites about things that you don't offer.

- Show your ads to people who are more likely to click them.

- Reduce costs by excluding keywords where you might be spending money but not getting a return.

- When you select negative keywords, you'll want to choose search terms that are similar to your keywords, but signal that people are looking for a different product.

When you set up your Google Adwords account, Google will offer you a free telephone consultation to help you get started. Make sure you take up this free consultation.

Webinars

A webinar is an online event that is hosted by you as the author and then broadcast to a select group of individuals through their computers via the Internet. A webinar is sometimes also referred to as a "webcast", "online event", or "web seminar".

A webinar allows you to share PowerPoint presentations, videos, web pages, or other multimedia content with your potential customers who can be located anywhere.

Webinars typically have audio and visual components. The visual component of a webinar is shared through a web conferencing tool or internet browser. The audio portion of a webinar is usually broadcast through the audience's computers (through speakers and media players) or through the telephone. Many authors are now using webinars as an effective way to provide details about their book(s) and how they will be of benefit to the reader. Of course, in order to hold a webinar you will need a list of potential customers to present it to, and this can be achieved by effective 'list-building', which I explained earlier. I usually run free webinars on a monthly basis, and it is not uncommon for me to sell upwards of 50 books per webinar that I run. There are a number of useful webinar software tools and platforms out there, and one in particular which is very popular is:

www.gotowebinar.co.uk

Google +

Google + is another great social platform for you to share your latest book(s) with your readers. As an author and publisher it is important for me to engage with my readers and customers through a variety of different channels and media. Google + is another great way that you can connect with your readers for free.

YouTube

I have found YouTube to be one of the most beneficial ways to promote my books free of charge. There are literally no advertising costs associated with YouTube, and you can start getting traffic to your book or website fast. In order to make it easier for you to understand how you can generate free traffic and sales for your book, allow me to provide you with a step-by-step tutorial. This is the exact same tutorial I use time and time again to promote my books.

STEP 1 – Write and publish your book. Once you have published your book you are now ready to start promoting it on YouTube.

STEP 2 – Open your YouTube account under your own author name, or alternatively with a name that is relevant to the genre or category your book falls under. For example, I decided to call my YouTube video account **'CareerVidz'** as it is a channel that is predominantly aimed at the under 25 job-seekers market.

STEP 3 – Create a short 10-15 minute video which is relevant to your book using **Camtasia Techsmith** or a similar software tool. The videos that I have created are presented on PowerPoint from my home computer. If you do not want to pay for the Camtasia Techsmith software then you could simply use your iphone or smartphone to record your video from home. For example, once I had published a book entitled 'MECHANICAL COMPREHENSION TESTS' I decided to create a short 10 minute video on this exact same subject. The video was educational and provided the viewer with important tips on how to prepare for this type of test. Here's the actual book I published to give you an idea what it looks like:

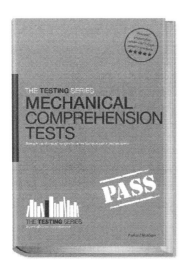

At the end of the video you should include one slide which directs people to either your website or Amazon, where they can buy your book.

STEP 4 – Once you have created and formatted your video, upload it to your YouTube channel. Make sure you title your video the same or similar to your book.

STEP 5 – Once you upload your video to your YouTube channel you then have the option to edit your video in the 'VIDEO MANAGER' and add 'ANNOTA-TIONS'. Sporadically during the content of the video I will add an annotation that encourages people to go to my website in order to download the book via the link that I include within the 'DESCRIPTION of the YouTube video.

The annotation for this particular video will read:

"Download my book at the link below!"

The video description will say:

DOWNLOAD Richard's Book HERE: **http://www.careervidz.com/ mechanical-comprehension-test-questions-and-answers.html**

You will note that I have included the full URL, including the extension 'http://' at the start of the link. If you do not include this, the link will not work.

Tip: If you do not have a website yet to promote your book, simply add the URL to your book on Amazon.

Tips for getting the most from your YouTube channel

1. Your YouTube videos must offer high-quality and engaging content as your viewers will have the opportunity to either give your video the 'thumbs-up' or the 'thumbs-down'. The more people who give it the thumbs-up, the more exposure YouTube will give your video in its ranking system. If lots of people give your video the thumbs' up the video will eventually rank on Google for the exact phrase of your video title. To prove my point, my 'MECHANICAL COMPREHENSION TESTS' video ranks on the first page of Google – this is all free traffic for my book.

2. Because YouTube is owned by Google, it is in your interests to use this media channel to promote your book, simply because you can get lots of free traffic for your book.

3. Once your video has been live for a few months and is generating plenty of 'thumbs-up', consider 'monetising' your video. Monetising your videos essentially means an advertisement will be played at the start of your YouTube video. Each time the advertisement gets played in full, you will get paid a commission. There are certain criteria and rules your video must meet before it can be eligible for monetisation, but it is something I strongly recommend you consider implementing.

4. You will have the opportunity to encourage people to 'subscribe' to your YouTube channel, too. At the time of writing my CareerVidz YouTube channel has received over 500,000 video views and has approximately 3,000 subscribers. These subscribers are all people I can contact at any time in the future to offer them my latest books and services.

Promoting my books on YouTube has proven to be a profitable way for me to sell my books to a wider audience, without the additional costs that can be involved with advertising.

CHAPTER 17
USEFUL LINKS AND RESOURCES

Get instant access to over 32 hours' worth of online training videos and support at:

www.BookPublishingAcademy.co.uk

USEFUL LINKS AND RESOURCES

Within this final chapter of the guide I have provided you with some links and resources which you may find useful.

ONLINE BOOK WRITING AND PUBLISHING TRAINING VIDEOS AND RESOURCES

www.BookPublishingAcademy.co.uk

BOOK AWARDS

www.costa.co.uk/costa-book-awards/welcome/

www.ipg.uk.com/awards

www.booktrust.org.uk/prizes/ - you can find out more about the following awards and prizes at this website:

- BBC National Short Story Award
- David Cohen Prize for Literature
- Independent Foreign Fiction Prize
- Kim Scott Walwyn Prize
- Sunday Times EFG Short Story Award
- Baileys Women's Prize for Fiction
- Blue Peter Book Awards
- The Booktrust Best Book Awards with Amazon Kindle
- Booktrust Best New Illustrators Award
- Children's Laureate
- Roald Dahl Funny Prize

HIGH-QUALITY BOOK COVER DESIGNER

www.SpiffingCovers.com

PRINTING COMPANY

www.Bell-Bain.com

SETTING UP GOOGLE PAY-PER-CLICK

www.nutpog.com

TIME MANAGEMENT COACH

www.AbigailBarnes.co.uk

VIDEO CREATION SOFTWARE TOOL

www.techsmith.com/camtasia.html

ECOOMERCE SHOPPING CARTS AND EMAIL MARKETING SYSTEMS

www.marketerschoice.co.uk

www.aweber.com

FREE WEBSITE BLOGS

www.blogger.com

www.weebly.com

www.wordpress.com

INDEPENDENT PUBLISHERS GUILD

www.ipg.uk.com

BOOK FAIRS

www.londonbookfair.co.uk/

www.bookfairs.scholastic.co.uk

www.poetrybookfair.com

ISBN NUMBERS

www.isbn.nielsenbook.co.uk

BAR CODE GENERATOR SOFTWARE

www.nchsoftware.com/barcode/

OUTSOURCING WEBSITES WHEREYOU CAN FIND GHOST-WRITERS, PROOFREADERS, EDITORS, BOOK DESIGNERS, TYPESETTERS AND EBOOK CONVERTORS

www.ODesk.com

www.Elance.com

www.99Designs.com

EBOOK CONVERSION FOR KINDLE

www.BookPublishingAcademy.co.uk

www.FingerPress.com

PACKAGING WEBSITES

www.davpack.co.uk

www.viking-direct.co.uk

CHEAP DELIVERY COURIERS

www.parcelmonkey.co.uk

NIELSEN BOOKDATA

www.nielsenbookdata.co.uk/

BOOK DISTRIBUTORS

www.gardners.com

KINDLE CONVERSION COMPANY

www.fingerpress.co.uk

STOCK IMAGE WESBITES

www.bigstockphoto.com

www.istockphoto.com

www.shutterstock.com

www.fotolia.com

COPYRIGHT AND INTELLECTUAL PROPERTY INFORMATION

www.ipo.gov.uk

www.start.biz

A FEW FINAL WORDS

You have now reached the end of the guide, but your authoring and publishing journey is only just beginning! I hope you have found the guide to be informative, helpful, and above all inspiring. Throughout my life I have always found a number of common factors in those people who achieve success. These are as follows:

1. They believe in themselves - the first factor in being a successful as an author and publisher is self-belief. Regardless of what anyone tells you, you can do it. Just like anything in life, you have to be prepared to work hard in order to be successful. Make sure you have the self-belief. Fill your mind with positive thoughts, and always ignore the doubters.

2. They choose to be successful - the second factor is choice. During my career I have been amazed at how many people have said to me that – "you are so lucky to have the life you do." My success is not down to luck, it is down to choice. I choose to work hard, and I want you to do the same, too.

3. They persevere - perseverance is my favourite word. Everybody comes across obstacles or setbacks in their life, but it is what you do about the setbacks that is important. View every setback as an opportunity; an opportunity for improvement and an opportunity to learn.

4. They have a mentor to guide and coach them - successful people will always have a mentor. That mentor will be instrumental in their success and will be the one person who helps them achieve the success they deserve.

To your success,

Richard McMunn

Richard McMunn

Get instant access to over 32 hours' worth of online training videos and support at:

www.BookPublishingAcademy.co.uk

If you would like me to personally mentor you to write your first book, please visit:

www.RichardMentorMe.com

For book writing and publishing training courses please go to:

www.BookPublishingCourses.com

21688858R00129

Printed in Great Britain
by Amazon